Ileana Alexandra O.

Staging Stalinism in Post-Communist Romanian Theatre

Cover design
by
Nic Ularu

Back cover
Yermolai Yepikhodov (Ovidiu Crişan) and Dunyasha (Vasilica Stamatin)
in Nic Ularu's staging of the play *The Cherry Orchard Sequel* at the
National Theatre "Lucian Blaga" in Cluj-Napoca

Copyright © Ileana Alexandra Orlich, 2012

Copyrights to the plays belong to the authors

ISBN 978-606-17-0191-9

Ileana Alexandra Orlich

Staging Stalinism in Post-Communist Romanian Theatre

casa cărții de știință
cluj-napoca, 2012

Acknowledgment

Publication of this book was made possible with support from the University of South Carolina, Columbia.

Many thanks to the National Theatre "Lucian Blaga" of Cluj-Napoca and to the "Bulandra" Theatre of Bucharest for permission to use pictures from their performances.

Contents

1. Preface

The Cultural Olympiad events inaugurated on April 23, Shakespeare's birthday, and celebrated in London around the 2012 Olympic Games, highlight theatre and theatrical performances as one of today's most enduring and enriching cultural legacies. Featured prominently in the festival, the Globe Theatre will be hosting all of Shakespeare's plays, each of which is to be performed by a different theatre company from around the world in its vernacular. According to the festival organizers, it's very interesting now to look at how people throughout the world see their own societies through the prism of Shakespeare, using the world to discuss Elizabethan Britain and its political intrigues four hundred years ago.

Conveying the same sense that the theatre offers a unique mode of cultural engagement with politics within a society, this book proposes to show how Romanian dramatists examine their society and politics through the prism of theatrical performance. While discussing three representative plays by dramatists born in Romania who at this time live in different cultural spaces – Vlad Zografi (Romania), Nic Ularu (the United States), and Matei Vişniec (France) – the critical essays in this book focus specifically on the engagement with politics and on the representation of totalitarian politics on Romanian contemporary stages during the turbulent history of a century highlighted by the Bolshevik Revolution, imposed Stalinism, and the rise and fall of Communism.

The three plays examined in this book indicate that

the Romanian post-Communist theatre manifests an abiding interest in Stalinist politics, possibly more than in traditional dramatic plot and character. After the collapse of the Berlin Wall and the end of an era dominated by Marxist-Leninist ideology, Romanian dramatists seek to appraise and understand the Communist period and simultaneously to demand a scrupulous and courageous recognition of all the irreconcilable antagonisms that made the lives of the people in Communism so burdensome and so desperate.

In examining some of these issues, I propose to show that Romanian contemporary theatre is an automatic by-product of being a playwright in a politically tormented century that feeds on the dead body of Communism and on an exhausted utopia. As it attempts to explain the different rhythms of separation with the country's Communist past, Romania's post-Communist theatre is an intellectually crowded space, unceasingly inventive, experimental, and porous in its engagement with politics.

2. *At Table with Marx*[1]

a poem by Matei Vişniec

1

We had been gobbling like pigs, heartily, our mouths craving for
sauces and seasonings,
our bellies were full and our eyes washed-out from glut
a light steam was billowing from the tablecloth, the
        crumbs were smoking
the empty glasses were gurgling, the knives thrust into
        bread rolls and meatballs
were vibrating gently extending the memory of the hand

it smelled of blood and minced meat, of vinegar and
        singed skin
of licked plates and of sweat
we were proud of ourselves after what had happened
history had sat with us at the table and now was dancing
        barefoot
on shards of broken glasses
we were proud of ourselves albeit a bit tired
right then the question was heard:
NOW WHO'S GOING TO WASH THE DISHES?

not me, said Marx
me neither, Engels's voice was heard
not me by any means, said Lenin

9

only Stalin was left, but Stalin had already fallen asleep
with his head between two dirty plates
and then it was me, the last comer, who had
in fact eaten the least, rather out of politeness

I looked in their eye – Marx, Engels, Lenin and Stalin had
in fact
a single eye mounted on a tank turret, an eye as big as a
lighthouse beacon
that rotated 360 degrees at every move of the bourgeoisie
I looked in their eye that was now vomiting blood
it was weird to see the blood of the working class boiling over
(like a cup of red milk forgotten on the gas burner)
I looked in their eye and in it I only saw myself
alone by a sink filled with black water
my hands sunk to the elbows into the black water
washing cups, plates and platters
and a lot of knives

2
I forgot to tell you that the table we had been eating at
stretched far into the horizon
and on the white tablecloth only my footprints could be seen
it's not easy being the youngest when a revolution begins
Lenin sends you for salt
you have no choice, you run to the horizon to fetch salt
Stalin sends you for mustard
what can you do, you crawl on your belly under the
grape clusters
dig a tunnel through the bread that obstructs your way
and get to the mustard jar
it's not that my boots had been dirty

10

on the tablecloth of history I only walk barefoot
but the saliva droplets and the rancid looks cast by the
        class enemies
will soil the soles of your feet in the end
that is the reason why the tablecloth
was now covered with bloody footmarks and all the land
        borders
were blunted almost to a cry

3
I know I'm speaking fast and I should have started from
        the end
but I've got a hundred million bodies to bury
and it's not easy to bury one hundred million dead when
        you suffer
from progressive myopia
no, it's not easy to bury one hundred million dead when
you dined with Marx until you turned 30
when you're left with such a bitter aftertaste in your mouth
when you have heartburns and throw up every five minutes

go figure, the blame's on me again, Marx and Engels are dozing
in the armchairs,
Lenin is having his tea, Stalin is smoking his pipe
and I must bury one hundred million dead
before dinner time

it's not easy to bury a hundred million dead
in just one mass grave
when you had lunch with them in the mass grave
when you were born with them in the mass grave, when
        you went to school with them
and you grew up with them in the mass grave
when you sang freedom songs with them

in the mass grave
the mouths that once sang in the choir
still risk singing while chewing earth

but most of all it's not easy to cover a mass grave
when all you have at your disposal are a sickle and a
        hammer
how can you dig a mass grave when you have at your
        disposal
only a sickle and a hammer and just a couple of hours
before the new history textbooks are coming out?

4

No, I shouldn't have dined with Marx,
now it is quite clear to me
I was wrong to sit at the table with Marx
I was wrong to sit at the table with Marx, Engels and
        Lenin
I shouldn't have eaten on the same tablecloth with them
I shouldn't have shared the bread and the salt with them
the same carafe of water and the same bottle of wine
I shouldn't have wished them bon appétit first, but I was
        hungry

no, I shouldn't have let Marx pass me the soup
I shouldn't have let Engels pass me the stewed cabbage
I shouldn't have let Lenin carve the meat
and above all I shouldn't have sat right in front of Stalin
when he eats, Stalin spatters awfully
now I smell of soup from head to toe, my hair is full of
        meat morsels
splattering out of Stalin's mouth
rivulets of sweat are trickling down my neck mixed

with saliva droplets sprung out of Stalin's mouth
and above the plate on which there is nothing left
now hovers a tune
a beautiful, touching love song
because, when he feels good, Stalin
sings even after his death

5
Epilogue
Good news: my birth has been postponed
I'll never be what I was destined to be
this is a certain thing, I'm on top of the world
nothing I was to live through will ever be lived
I'll have another past and another future
I'll have another relation with God, with evil and good
I'll lose at other games, I'll fall in love with other women
and maybe I won't be a man anymore
maybe I'll experience the mystery of birth too
I didn't know it was possible but
lo, the moment you die everything is possible.

How to Read Post-Communist Theatre:

Matei Vişniec's *At Table with Marx*

Communism, which developed out of Karl Marx's romantic enthusiasm and scientific theories[2] and of Lenin's resentment[3], came to Romania from outside, as a kind of intruder; or, it could also be said that Romanians were late comers to the table that Marx, Engels, Lenin and Stalin set up – a table whose ideological feast that extended from Berlin to Moscow left in its wake over one hundred million human lives, according to one of the captions in the Warsaw Museum of Communism.

Conceptualized like a dramatic monologue focused on pre- and post-Stalinism, Vişniec's poem *At Table with Marx* acts out the historical drama of Communism and the challenge to Marxist orthodoxy as a tripartite process unfolding in the liveliness and concision of three acts: the meal with all its trimmings; the washing of the dishes under a cyclopic eye, both self-reflexive and watchful, to suggest an overpowering helplessness and a search for identity as a place to project and express what is missing in one's maimed identity; and the traumatic participation that resulted in the formation of post-Communist identity announced in the poem's *Epilogue*. Disguising humorously the personalized calamities and barren struggles against ideological oppression of the poet-protagonist's autobiographical self, *At Table with Marx* also illustrates the poor anti-totalitarian resistance, the dubious dignity of survival and the problematic moral choices inside an endless cycle of political repression and

14

totalitarian control that made a prison house of the whole society.[4]

In the beginning, one believed in the Marxist utopia that united the voices of Marx and Engels, but then was disappointed by the brutality of Lenin's Bolshevik agenda and the socialist reality of Stalin's excesses, which ended in a totalitarian nightmare operating through an apparatus of terror and control over any thought, any opinion, and any deed done or undone. In Vișniec's poem, the simple story of daily life in Communist Romania is visualized at first by means of a feast, with "sauces and seasonings" and "bread rolls and meat balls," and the ensuing feeling that "history had sat with us at the table and now was dancing barefoot [making us] proud of ourselves after what had happened." Among other things, what had happened was an appropriation of evil that had become part of the daily practices and had spread endemically to become second nature to all those eating at the same table with Marx, Engels, Lenin and Stalin.

The second phase, the dish washing that entailed the internalization of evil, calls for images of disfigurement with the eye featured prominently: "Marx, Engels, Lenin and Stalin had in fact a single eye mounted on a tank turret, an eye as big as a lighthouse beacon that rotated 360 degrees at every move of the bourgeoisie." Vișniec seems to insert here the fetish for eye, well represented in Romanian modernity, particularly in the works of Victor Brauner, one of the celebrated artists of the Romanian avant-garde exiled in Paris between the two wars, who famously declared that "For years, I painted topics concerning eyes. Exchanged, destroyed, distorted, disproportionate, replaced, destroyed eyes, for years and years you could see eyes in my paintings or drawings."[5]

Having exhausted his gaze into the eye vomiting

blood of Marx, Engels, Lenin and Stalin, the poet realizes that he sees in it his own image. In the line "I looked in their eye and in it I only saw myself," the dissolution of epistemological coherence boils down to the understanding that self-knowledge is impossible. The giant eye shows Vişniec as a subject symbolically frozen in front of the Medusa-like portrait of Marx, Engels, Lenin and Stalin. He appears as a petrified mirror of himself that tells the story of the unbearable nature of an event and the story of the unbearable nature of the poet's survival in a loop of repugnance that puts him in a fragile, liminal situation. By looking at his own hollow eye mirrored in the eyes of Marx, Engels, Lenin and Stalin, the poet is forced to see himself at the brink of extinction, of a blackness that threatens and disturbs his sense of order. Its presence in his life does not radically cut him off from what threatens him; on the contrary, the blackness keeps him in the proximity of utter abjection, a hopelessness which combines ambiguity and perpetual danger.

Placing himself in the vicinity of such visions, Vişniec seems to acknowledge his belief in a world that was in the blind spot, beyond pure sight. Unlike Brauner, whose painting of eyes as surrealist motifs showed that the mind was deactivated in order to reach a deeper realm, Vişniec is closer to Luis Buñuel's vision in the short silent film *Le chien andalou* which featured a close-up with a young woman's left eye about to be slit by a razor. Like Buñuel who imagines surreal mutilation, Vişniec's eye summons the conceptual essence of a bloody dictatorship and an aberrant ideology, which soon becomes "a sink filled with black water" where "hands sunk to the elbows into the black water wash[ing] cups, plates and platters and a lot of knives." The culmination of Communism comes with the matter-of-fact burial of "a hundred million dead in just one mass grave" that refuse to let go and keep company to the living who can't really bury them with only "a sickle and a hammer." The Real, that is, the materiality of the bodies, overshadows and destabilizes the meaning of the symbolic order announced by the emblematic signs of the proletarian and the peasant classes, united in achieving a happy destiny for the Communist nation – the successful industrialization and collectivization.

In a sinister register that resonates with the banality of evil, the burial appears as a common occurrence, like the dusting of furniture, carried out by a desensitized individual. With courage and public commitment sublimated or diverted to pseudo-resistance, human life is no longer valued, and resistance through culture, offering "neither too much resistance nor enough culture," is left to summon a spiritual Waste Land in the burial of the dead. Or, transfixed in a different type of cultural register, the putative common grave for one hundred million dead is "a hammered place, a place where Communism left its deepest trails"[6] in an extended Soviet Kremlin filled up with decomposed bodies in all its niches.

As the poet facetiously confesses, dining with Marx, Engels and Lenin was the wrong thing to do, even if Stalin, the latest addition to the commanding table, eventually began to indulge in the tune of a beautiful love song for those who were still left to listen. The washing of the dishes appears to be the domestic equivalent to expiation and atonement, for having accepted the soup, the stewed cabbage, and the carved meat passed by Marx, Engels and Lenin, and for having sat "right in front of Stalin."

What makes the atonement singular in Vişniec's poem is the total absence of any kind of anti-Communist motivation. The poem simply records a collective memory by means of an open and humorous confession

17

of collaborative participation from all the people who lived under Communism, under an ideology imposed through power and control. As a necessary element in the healing process, the collective memory not only liberates from the ghost of the past, but also protects the present from possible blackouts, allowing for the rebirth of the poet-protagonist in the post-Communist era.

Ultimately, the post-Communist experience is attached to the cultural horizon of remembering a lost utopia articulated through the medium of irony and humor. What this means is that if Communism was utopian, then the past remains nothing more than a cultural era, with its memorabilia that include Marx, Engels, Lenin and Stalin neatly stacked, like the Matryosha dolls. In such a context, the entire space of the historical, political, moral and theoretical experience of Communism was not a political condition, but only and exclusively a cultural space engendering today's post-Communist discourse.

In post-Communist Romania, which heralds a newly-born democracy and in which culture has become a place for forgetting (with Communism as merely "another past"), one must find a new identity that separates the self from the past. Thus the poet announces his own birth, another relation with God, the promise of new love, and the endless possibilities he contemplates from the "top of the world." But he is also mindful that the past engagement while at table with Marx, Engels, Lenin and Stalin, cannot and must not be forgotten, if one is to understand the moral purposes of the poet-protagonist's impassioned plea and to measure the validity of his dramatic monologue by the standards of poetic justice.

Timofei (Lucian Rad), one of the patients in Vişniec's *How to Teach the History of Communism to Mental Patients* in Mona Chirilă's staging of the play at the National Theatre "Lucian Blaga" in Cluj-Napoca

Notes

1. Vişniec's poem *La Masă cu Marx* was published recently in Romania in the volume of the same title (Bucureşti: Cartea Românească. 2011). The English translation is mine.

2. In the Warsaw Museum of Communism, Marx's caption explains that "Communists justify the practice of revolutionary terror and dictatorship of the proletariat with the alleged irrefutability of the 'scientific' theories of Karl Marx, the bohemian and intellectual adventurer, who started his career as a romantic poet with a tendency to apocalyptic idealism. He studied Hegelian philosophy and after that became a sharp-edged journalist with a focus on economical and political affairs."

3. The text accompanying Lenin's exhibit in the same museum states that "The chief cause of his irreconcilable hatred against the establishment was the death of his older brother, who was executed because of an attempted murder of the Tsar. From the beginning, Lenin tried to enforce the tactics of betrayal and relentlessness that became characteristics of the Communist regime."

4. See Heinrich Boll on the dialectic between free prisoners and the imprisoned society in "The Imprisoned World of Solzhenitsyn's *The First Circle*," *Aleksandr Solzhenitsyn: Critical Essays and Documentary Materials*. Eds. J. B. Dunlop, R. S. Haugh, and Michael Nicholson. Stanford:Hoover Institution Press,1985. 219-30.

5. Brauner, Victor. *Cahier 1944*, 32. (*J'ai peint pendant des années des sujets ou il y avait des yeux. Des yeux changes, détruits, difforme, disproportionnés, remplacés, anéantis pendant des années dans mes tableaux ou dessins on pouvait voir des yeux.*)

6. For a detailed description and analysis of "The Post-Communist Condition or the Various Speeds of Separation from the Past," see Marius Babias, "The Euro-Self and the Europeanism" in *Genealogies of Communism*, Cluj: Editura Idea Design and Print, 2009. 253-269.

3. Specters of State Power, History, and Politics of the Stage:

Reading Vlad Zografi's *Peter or The Sun Spots*

Written in the aftermath of the political upheaval triggered by the fall of the Berlin Wall, Vlad Zografi's play *Peter or The Sun Spots* brings to the stage an intriguing historical perspective on the great tsar credited with modernizing a backward country. While staging the proximities between the political and the aesthetic, the play also invites through dramatic inferences the uncanny compatibility between Peter, the White Tsar who reigned from 1682 to 1725 with the iron hand of the autocrat through the vast realm of his empire, and Stalin, the Red Tsar whose long tenure in the Kremlin, from 1928 until his death in 1953, brought to fruition the agenda of the Bolshevik Revolution.

Articulated in terms of interactions and relations between Europe's East and West, the play captures on an immediate level Peter's despotic and depraved behavior during his visit to France and, in dramatically recognizable scenes that foreshadow Stalin's autocratic system, suggests a direct lineage from the tsar to the leader known throughout the Soviet Union as the Man of Steel. .

While Zografi's views mark the political opening made possible by the emergence of democratic Central European countries in the former Soviet bloc after forty-five years of enforced Communism, the dramatic performance highlights a political "Peter with Stalin" pairing, analogous to the one Lacan institutes in his 1963 essay "Kant with Sade." A reading of Kenneth Reinhard's essay on Lacan's startling exploration of the "with" in the juxtaposition of Kant/Sade locating Sade not at the antipodes of an Enlightenment mapped out by the morality of Kant, but as its "seamy yet continuous other side" (796),[1] leads in turn to interesting perspectives in which, through the conjunctures of Zografi's play, Peter reveals hidden truths not only about himself but also about Stalin, precisely in what Reinhard calls the non-reciprocity or asymmetrical substitution of their relationship. Specifically, Zografi's revelation of perversions associated with Peter the Great during his visit to France, as in the unveiling of the underside of Enlightenment in the "Kant with Sade," is predicated on the "Peter with Stalin" conjuncture based not only on historical congruities, but also on the critical act through which Peter and Stalin hold interchangeable roles, or "neighbor" on each other, and thus articulate an ideal material of "comparative study otherwise than comparison," complicated by history, politics and theatrical aesthetics. Further, coming from distinct traditions but aiming at similar ends, the neighboring of Peter and Stalin is a paradigm for negotiating the subjectivity of Peter's dramatic persona in relation not only to late-medieval Russia vis-à-vis France but mainly in the linear temporality of historical causality with the twentieth-century Soviet Union. In this context, Zografi's play is an imaginary screen that dissimulates in dramatic terms the relationship between the self (Peter/Stalin) and the other (Russia/Russians) articulated through the

22

protective circulation of fantasy weaved around the structural impasse of Orthodoxism in late-medieval and modern Russia. Borrowing once again from the extended implications of Reinhard's reading of Lacan with Levinas,[2] in the critical act through which one (con)text takes the place of another, the Peter/Stalin structural isomorphism directs the play onto a non-reciprocal or asymmetrical counter-reading of the imperative commandment to "love thy neighbor as thyself" that unites Russia's Orthodox Church in the difficult conjunction with tsarist/Stalinist autocracy.

For Zografi the ongoing compulsion to return to the East West dichotomies in general, and to Stalin in particular, is predicated on personal experiences, notably his extended stay in the USSR and in Paris as a doctoral student. Having also witnessed the demise of Communism in his native Romania and the changes occurred in the country by 1996, the year when he wrote *Peter*, Zografi foregrounds in the play repressed political and historical truths by staging a gripping interrogation of the White Tsar's autocracy, despotism, expansionist tendencies and expressed desire to catch up with Western Europe and by suggesting their implicit compatibility with Stalin's nationalist agenda and totalitarian politics. As the play unveils in Peter's Russia a culture very much attracted by the idea of the nation-state, a place where the Orthodox Church plays an irrationally strong role, where secret services and spies play an important part in the society and where people tend to behave quite irrationally in submissive and degrading ways, the field of signification opens to reveal the reciprocity between Peter's Russia and Stalin's USSR as "the echo of a sound that would precede the resonance of this sound."[3]

The historical Peter was a traveler who had seen Amsterdam, London, Berlin and Vienna by the time he decided to go to Paris in 1717 with a large retinue of sixty-one, twenty-two persons of rank and thirty-nine orderlies. Zografi's play, which is based on this visit to Paris, has little to do with the official reports of the time, particularly Saint-Simon's writings detailing the tsar's visit and his own meeting with Peter, which the play mentions in a preamble. Instead, Zografi uses Peter's well documented visit to turn the Russian tsar into a subject firmly situated in the interplay of what Jacques Rancière in *The Politics of Aesthetic* calls a 'poetic' story or 'history' that links realism with artificialism to assemble the montage of our complex understanding.[4] Devoted to the 'real,' the play is in this sense capable of greater invention than fiction as it fictionalizes Peter not by making him into a fictional character but by playing off the combination of different types of traces in order to suggest the possibilities for the thinking of Peter's story or of the history of Russia and the common perceptions about Russia in general, and of Zografi's contemporary USSR in particular.

Throughout the play, the real is fictionalized in order to be thought. Archival information or extracts from historical accounts, such as Robert K. Massie's *Peter the Great: His Life and World* (1981),[5] provide the documented names of Peter's party during his trip to Paris, including Golovkin, Shafirov, Peter Tolstoy, Vasily Dolgoruky, Buturlin, Osterman and Yaguzhinsky, or such incidents as Peter's refusal to take up residence in the luxurious apartments of the Queen Mother and his insistence on being quartered at the Hôtel Lesdiguières, whose garden could be seen from the tower windows of the Bastille. It is entirely possible that during the weeks Peter spent strolling among the trees of the hotel's garden, a famous Frenchman locked in the Bastille, the twenty-three-year-old François-Marie Arouet, looked down and saw the tsar's frequent walks. Forty years later, using the name Voltaire, this prisoner would write a *History of the Russian Empire under Peter the Great.* Affronted by Peter's behavior and his numerous unsupervised outings conducted without ceremony throughout the city, the French felt that the tsar not only displayed "a haughty air of superiority" but that he also behaved "without any civility"(Massie, 642) – a perception on which Zografi's play capitalizes to portray the tsar's character.

Since writing history and writing stories come under the same regime of truth, Zografi relies on recorded events that allow for the dramatic displays of the play's pervasive political intentionality. Among such documented occurrences that link Peter with Stalin are Peter's visit to the vast hospital and barracks of the Invalides where the tsar, in uncanny anticipation of Stalinism's rhetoric that captures the farcical relationship between subjects and Soviet authority, called the 4,000 disabled soldiers his "comrades" (Massie, 648) and Peter's conversation at the Sorbonne with a group of Catholic theologians who gave him a plan for the reunification of the Eastern (Orthodox) and Western (Catholic) churches. Peter took the plan with him back to Russia, where he ordered his Russian bishops to study it and give him an opinion, which he subsequently never solicited from them. His rule, the rule of the autocrat in all matters, was supreme and absolute; ordained priests of the Orthodox

Church, unlike prelates in the West, were required to swear an oath pledging themselves "to defend unsparingly all powers, rights and prerogatives belonging to the High Authority of His Majesty" (Massie, 793).

Apart from such historical evidence underscoring Zografi's historical documentation, Peter's assertive identity in the play is shared in a "relational way" that enables "a double avoidance of self-sameness and total estrangement, responding to Barbara's Stafford's recent plea in *Visual Analogy: Consciousness as the Art of Connecting*.[6] As a subject embedded in a network of partial others alongside his own entourage, the French court, the philosopher de la Manque, and the prostitute Coco, the tsar is not an isolated ruler; Zografi's dramatic logic of differential degrees of likeness provides the foundation for not only the collapse of Peter's isolation as a subject in the play, but also for a less confrontational reconfiguration of the compatible or comparable identities of Peter and, implicitly, of Stalin, and of the Russian and French cultures, with the play acting as a guide to the potential of such a separation-in-jointness of the white and the red tsars. To be sure, theirs is not a new-age harmony; however, in implying a relational jointness of Peter with Stalin, the play blurs the border between the logic of facts and the logic of fiction to create a model for the fabrication of stories linked to a certain idea of history as common destiny, on Russia as a locus of political and religious relationship formation and on Peter's reign as a foundational moment for all future autocratic rule and patrilineage guaranteeing Orthodoxy the role of state religion in the Russian empire.

Scene from the French court at the time of Tsar Peter's visit in Catalina Buzoianu's
1998 staging of the play *Peter* at the Bulandra Theatre in Bucharest

The opening of the play, which offers a panoramic view
of an open market in Paris where Peter's spies, Ivan
Semyonovich Shalyapin and Dimitri Alexeyevich Smirnov,
are mingling with the crowds and the merchants, stages the
differences between East and West. The two spies' regrets at
not having in a long time had the chance "to castrate a
heretical priest, or grill a rioter, or cut off a nun's tits" (23),[7]
as well as their encounters with the merchants and
assessment of French perfumes and other products available
at "the lousy marketplace in Parizh" (23), allow for the
play's reach outside, beyond the immediate scene, to
suggest the notion of Russian and French nationality in
early-eighteenth century, with specific patterns that evolved
into our own: the kinship of a population and the definition

of foreign. The dramatic intervention of the political or the system of division and boundaries that define what is visible and audible with a particular aesthetico-political regime, is gleaned in such exchanges as those of the French Duke's statement that "France is much richer than you can imagine. France is a big country" and the courtier Olivier's response that "Russia is a thousand times bigger" (27), or in the Duke's arrogant acknowledgment that the French will conquer the world not through philosophy or engineering but by "gorge[ing] everybody chockfull with our gastronomic culture and asphyxiate[ing] them with our perfumes" (29).

Not unlike Paris, Moscow was in Peter's time a space with a brawling, open-air marketplace, with rows and rows of shops and wood stalls teeming and reverberating around a Red Square different from the silent, cobbled streets one finds today beneath the fantastic, clustered steeples and cupolas of St. Basil's the Blessed Cathedral and the Kremlin walls. Then it was filled with merchants shouting at customers to step up and inspect their wares, the velvet, brocade, Persian and Armenian silk, bronze, brass and copper goods, iron wares, tooled leather, pottery and innumerable objects made of wood, offering a different kind of trade from the French refineries Peter's spies disdain. In both places, there were also women like the play's Coco, who in addition to goods, might be selling another commodity, and who located their customers as easily and readily as Coco finds Peter.

Early in the play, the French courtiers report on the Russian tsar who scandalizes the French court with his course manners, such as snatching watches from the corset of French countesses, and unthinkable stinginess.

28

Politics plays itself out in the theatrical paradigms as meaning produced by the actors' bodies, the imaginary stories, or the functions of speech. Peter's behavior toward Coco, the prostitute he humiliates and for whose services he refuses to pay adequately, actualizes his power in the very act of signaling his discretionary authority. To document Peter's behavior in the play Zografi did not have to look any further than to such historical accounts as Peter's 1716 visit to Copenhagen, Denmark. The recorded incident which focuses on King Frederic IV's smiling remark to Peter, "I hear you also have a mistress," has Peter snapping back to say that "my harlots do not cost me much, but yours cost you thousands of pounds which could be better spent" (Massie, 811).

Scene from the French court at the time of Tsar Peter's visit in Catalina Buzoianu's 1998 staging of the play *Peter* at the Bulandra Theatre in Bucharest

Peter's reason for the visit to France, apart from the stated plan "to civilize Russia," becomes soon apparent in the play. Working behind the scenes, his "most skilled agents," Shalyapin and Smirnov, are on a mission to find the philosopher Pierre de la Manque, whose brain Peter wishes to pick in trying to find out how he "can change the Russian people" (55). After accidentally stumbling into de la Manque, Peter becomes very unhappy with the cynic philosopher's stubborn proclamations that "Russia is an unhealthily big country" (52) and that nothing can be done to change Russia and Russians and, finally, with de la Manque's comment that the tsar would not be able to lead the Russians as he does should they be able to change. Infuriated by de la Manque's crude evaluations, Peter orders his courtiers to murder him because, as tsar of all Russians, Peter does not want such dangerous assessments of his people, and of himself as supreme Majesty, to be known.

In acting out an imaginary punishment, Zografi literalizes the tsar's alleged power and, through extension, that of Stalin, as Peter's murder of La Manque at the hands of his loyal courtiers bears all the marks of Stalin's treatment of those he perceived to be dangerous. Roughly two hundred years after Peter's visit in Paris, in 1918, when the Bolsheviks were struggling for survival, Lenin deployed Stalin to Tsaritsyn, the key strategic city on the Lower Volga, the gateway to the grain and oil of the North Caucasus, and the southerly key to Moscow, which was in danger of falling to the Whites. Stalin showed he meant business by shooting any suspect counter-revolutionaries in the city. During those days, as an answer to Trotsky whom Stalin considered "an operetta commander, a chatter box," Stalin is meant to have also said: "Death solves all problems. No man, no problem." This simply was Stalin's way, as attested in more recent accounts like Simon Sebeg Montefiore's *Stalin: The Court of the Red Tsar* (2003), a book which details the horrors of Stalinism beyond the Gulag, complete with Lavrenti Beria's yearly quota of 75,950 executions in the early 1930's (later to be raised), the beating to death of Stalin's political foes' teenage children, and the torture of the widows by placing snakes in their prison cells.

Clothed in fictional referentiality, the brutal murder of de la Manque in Zografi's play reveals Peter's criminal streak that the tsar casually acknowledges when he tells Shalyapin that he has "treaded on mountains of corpses. Sometimes I with my own hand" (74). De la Manque's murder saddens Peter's jester, Nikita Zotov, a character patterned after the real Nikita Zotov, a clerk in the tax-collection department of Tsar Fedor, Peter's half-brother, appointed as tutor to the five-year old Peter by his widowed mother, Tsaritsa Natalya Naryshkina. (There is a slight discrepancy in the play, with Zotov saying that he's known Peter since the boy was ten.) As in Zografi's play, which features a likable pope-prince in the jester who is often asked to pose as the tsar, Nikita Zotov was an amiable, literate man whom Peter kept close for as long as the tutor lived. Although not a scholar, Zotov taught Peter the alphabet, the Bible (which the future tsar could still recite by heart forty years later), and above all prepared his young pupil to be open and curious, in short to grow into the self-taught man that Peter was to become as a tsar.

In credible fashion given the historical Peter's relationship with Zotov, Peter turns to Zotov, the only man he trusts in the play, to express his horror at discovering spots in the sun with the telescope the French academicians allow him to use. The discovery of the "shameful disease of the sun," forces Peter to see that not only are Russians backward in relation to the West's advanced sciences, but also that their deep-seated belief in the greatness of their tsar, associated in Russian proverbs with the perfection of a glorious and eternal sun, is severely challenged and undermined. For, as Peter acknowledges when he remarks in horror that "if this sun dies, we pass away too, we'll conk like a pack of rats" (70), if the sun is imperfect and subject to extinction, so are the tsar and his unlimited power.

The close cultural association of the tsar with the sun is signaled in state documents and in proverbs to which, in Peter's spy Shalyapin's contemptuous comment in the play, "Russians cling." Before Peter's time, the embassy of Englishmen sent to Russia in 1664 to thank Peter's father, Tsar Alexis, for his constant support of the once-exiled monarch, Charles II, captures this august figure as remote and forever inaccessible to his subjects in his splendid magnificence:

> The Tsar like a sparkling sun darted forth most sumptuous rays, being most magnificently placed upon his throne, with his scepter in hand and having his crown on his head. His throne was of massy silver gilt, wrought curiously on top with several works and pyramids; and being seven or eight steps higher than the floor, it rendered the person of the Prince transcendently majestic. (Massie, 9)

A few centuries later, in the USSR, Stalin was perceived in similar ways as the sky's most luminous globe, a notion most Soviets embraced, especially since it had been immortalized in M. Isakovski, "Song of Stalin". Written in 1936, at the height of Stalin's autocracy, the popular lines of Isakovski, a Russian poet, a laureate of two USSR State Prizes (1943, 1949), and a Hero of Socialist Labor (1970), proclaimed the heavenly power of Stalin, the Sun-trusted leader:

> And strength and youth and glory/ He gave us for eternal time/ He kindled bright spring sunrises/ Over our homesteads./ Comrades, we sing a song/ To that most trusted man_/ Of the sun, the truth of peoples,/ Of Stalin we sing a song. *(Bolshaya Sovietskaya Encyclopedia)*

From times immemorial, proverbs like "One sun shines in heaven and the Russian tsar on earth" teach Russians to regard their ruler as a god-like or sun-like creature from infancy. The rhetoric of proverbs ("Only God and the tsar know," "Through God and the tsar, Russia is strong") also indicate the tsar's influence and authority and relate the Russians' feeling for the tsar and for their land. In a sense, long before Communism, the Russian land was communal. It belonged to the tsar as father, but also to the people, his family, as in "The sovereign is the father, the earth the mother." The ruler was the tsar who could dispose of Russia's riches, yet the country still remained the joint property of the national family. The tsar, in this familial scheme, was the father, his autocratic rule was patriarchal. He had unlimited power over his subjects, the same as a father has over his

33

children, and the Russian people could not have imagined any limitation of the power of the tsar that, as the proverbs show, seemed to seep in unnoticeably and to manifest itself psychologically.

Throughout the play the spies' fear of and servile attitude toward Peter, as well as their interactions with the French court, reveal moral, social and cultural characteristics of the Russians, a true and eternal people Peter and later Stalin ruled autocratically. There were agents everywhere in Peter's Russia, watching and listening, reporting to the tsar any "violent and unseemly speech." The height of this practice reached its apogee in 1702, when Peter created the Secret Office, with jurisdiction over all crimes and especially treason by "word or deed." Any suggestion of treason or rebellion was immediately reported through a network of pervasive eavesdropping and denunciation, followed by torture and execution of the suspects, a system foreshadowing in every way Stalin's NKVD and the terror of the Gulag and Lubianka. (Further testimony to this practice in more recent times can be found in Joseph Conrad's *Under Western Eyes*, a novel which details the devastating consequences of the infiltrating job carried out by tsarist Russia's specialized network of spies in the lives of the characters, particularly the tragic protagonist Razumov.)

Unlike Westerners engaged in Peter's time into the advancing sciences and the formulation of democratic principles through the Renaissance and Reformation, and into the Enlightenment, Russia, her church and her rulers remained pure and petrified in their primeval past. The weight and strain of this cultural backwardness began to take its toll on Russian society as later, in the twentieth century, Stalin's suspicion toward foreigners and the West reflected the nation's collective sentiment and the Soviet people's acceptance of a rule of the land that offered little satisfaction and allowed for no democratic institutions, an unconditional acceptance of a political and social oppression that appealed to them in ways more powerful than rebellious logic and cold reasoning.

Russians bowed unconditionally to the ritual, dogma and practices of Orthodoxy emancipated from the primacy of Constantinople in 1589, when the office of the first Patriarch of Moscow was created. Moscow and Russia had thus early on achieved independence – and isolation. Confronted on the south by the Islamic Turks and Tartars, on the north by Lutheran Sweden and on the west by Catholic Poland from whom Peter's grandfather had snatched the city of Kiev and Ukraine, the Russian church adopted and in turn disseminated a defensive stance of xenophobic conservatism. All change became abhorrent, and huge energies were devoted to the exclusion of foreign influences and scientific thought.

Aware of the collective power of the church reproduced in all the Russians who made themselves subject to it, Peter fought to subordinate the church to the state and promoted those supporting his political objective to have the clergy, like the army, the civil administration or the artisans subject to the tsar's power. Ultimately, Peter abolished the one-man rule of the Patriarch and replaced it with a collective administration, the Holy Synod abiding by the Ecclesiastical Regulations. By abolishing the Patriarchate and transforming the administration of the church into a branch of the secular government Peter could finally rule over Russia as an absolute monarch, whose power was given to him by God.

Deeply ingrained in the Russian soul, Christianity defined in the commandment to "love thy neighbor as thyself" (Leviticus 19:18), as determined and exemplified by St. Augustine,[8] united the Orthodox Russians by mutual identification grounded in the reflexivity of self-love. It is however, the imperative of this interpretation against the incommensurability of the injunction's three basic terms, the neighbor, self, and love that receives special attention in the writings of Emanuel Levinas. In *Otherwise than Being, or Beyond Essence*,[9] Levinas reformulates the Biblical call to neighbor-love as the insistence on a relation to the other that antedates the very being of the subject. The neighbor names the occasion of an originary responsibility that precedes both the subject who assumes that obligation and the community in which responsibility will be represented. In a 1982 interview Levinas comments that "responsibility for the neighbor" is doubtless "the strict term for that which is called the love of the neighbor"[10], insofar as both are defined by an ability to respond to the other that is not predicated on the experience of self-love (as in St. Augustine) but is rather the precondition of the self. Levinas argues that the subject as such (in this case the tsar) is "called into being" finding itself obsessed with its neighbor (the Russians):

> The neighbor (Russians) concerns the tsar before all assumption, all commitment, consented or refused. Russians are bound to him, their tsar, who is, however, the first one on the scene, not

36

signaled, unparalleled; I, the tsar, am bound to the Russians, before any liaison, contracted. ... Here there is a relation of kinship outside of all biology, "against all logic." It is not because the Russians would be recognized as belonging to the same genius as the tsar that they concern him. He, the tsar, is precisely *other*. The community with the tsar begins in the Russians' obligation to him.[11]

Interpreting such lines in terms of Russian Orthodoxy, the subject's, i.e., the tsar's, responsibility for the people, the Russians, as his neighbor forms the basis of their community. In this context, the subject, who is the tsar, or later Stalin, becomes an integral and absolute ego individual, unique and irreplaceable, whose business is the absolute. No one can substitute himself for the tsar, who substitutes himself for all.

Further, the uniqueness of the tsar as self lies not in his identity, but in the singularity and infinity of his responsibility to this people; no one can replace him in his obligation to his neighbor/his people. Moreover, because this responsibility is singular and not transferable, it can never be reciprocal; the tsar has one more obligation than anyone else insofar as he is not only responsible for the neighbor, the Russians, but also responsible for *the other's/Russians' responsibility*.

These observations make a lot of sense in the context of de la Manque's assessment in the play of Russians as a people who cannot change and thus can only be ruled.

In his Talmudic reading from 1982, "The Pact," Levinas renders the injunction to "Love thy neighbor as thyself" as "Be responsible for the other as you are responsible for yourself," a formulation that reverses and upsets the reflexive arc implied by the verse's Augustinian translation.[12] Whereas love of the neighbor circles from subject to the other and back, responsibility for the neighbor may originate in love or *as a traumatic response to the other* (my italics); the relationship between self and neighbor is reciprocal but not symmetrical. The trauma of asymmetry may also take religion as its defense mechanism.

Further, despite the structures of social representations attempting to establish "reciprocal relations" of the Russians with the tsar, the tsar assumes a responsibility for the Russians that is not mutual, that cannot be amortized, and that is in fact infinitely asymmetrical. As supreme ruler, with divine rights, the more he answers the more he is responsible; the more he approaches the Russians with which he is encharged, the further away he is. Lastly, his responsibility for the Russians cannot reciprocally entail their responsibility for him; on the other hand, for the tsar to require the Russians to indebt themselves to him would be to ask for human sacrifice – hence the expectation, in the deferred spatiality and temporality of the play, to die for the tsar or Stalin by choosing to follow the presumed expectations of the all-pervasive tsarist or Stalinist power aimed, ironically, at the slow destruction of the Russians' resistance and self-worth vis-à-vis the god-like ruler's self-assertion and commands.

Based on this paradigm, Russia is a country of command and obedience system, where the only agency is that of that of autocratic rule and where no provisions are made for democratic governance or religious stewardship. Today, however, the exhaustion of the Communist utopia in the former Soviet bloc admits that the post-Communist present has been filtered through the agonizing body of Communism as a last community utopia with universalist aspirations.

Notes

1. Lacan, Jacques. "Kant avec Sade." In *Écrits*. Paris: Seuil, 1966. 765-790. Trans. As "Kant with Sade" by James B. Swenson, Jr. *October* 51 (Winter 1989). 55-75.

2. Reinhard, Kenneth. "Kant with Sade, Lacan with Levinas." In MLN, Vol. 110, No. 4. Comparative Literature Issue (Sept. 1995). 785-808.

3. Lacan, Jacques. "Kant avec Sade." 793.

4. Rancière, Jacques. *The Politics of Aesthetics: The Distribution of the Sensible*. Trans. Gabriel Rockhill. London: Continuum, 2004. 38.

5. Massie, Robert K., *Peter the Great: His Life and World*. New York: Ballantine Books, 1980.

6. Stafford, Barbara. *Visual Analogy: Consciousness as the Art of Connecting*. Cambridge: MIT P, 2001. 10, 86.

7. Zografi. Vlad *Kiss me: Confessions of a Bare Footed Leper*. Bettie Youngs Book Publishers. Gardena: California, 2011. All quotations are from this edition of the book.

8. Augustine, Saint. *On Christian Doctrine*. Trans. D. W. Robertson, Jr. Indianapolis: Bobbs-Merril, 1958.

9. Lévinas, Emmanuel. *Autrement qu'être ou au-delà de l'essence*. Paris: Kluwer Academic (Livre de Poche), 1974. Trans. Alphonso Lingis as *Otherwise Than Being or Beyond Essence*. Boston: Kluwer Academic Publishers, 1991.

10. _____. *Entre nous: essays sur le penser-à-l'autre*. Paris: Grasset (Livre de Poche), 1991. 113.

11. _____. *Otherwise than Being*, 87.

12. _____. *Beyond the Verse: Talmudic Readings and Lectures*. Trans. Gary D. Mole. Bloomington: Indiana University P, 1994. 84.

4. The Political Ghosts and Ideological Phantasms of Nic Ularu's

The Cherry Orchard Sequel

Emphasized as in Chekhov's title, the cherry orchard is the primary metaphor in Nic Ularu's *The Cherry Orchard Sequel*, a play that premiered at the La MaMa Etc. Theatre in New York on February 21, 2008. To a certain extent, then, Ularu's text (mentioned henceforth as *A Sequel*) is a predictable manipulation of the characters' actions after the moment when Chekhov's aggressive parvenu Yermolai Alekseyevich Lopakhin takes over the cherry orchard and allows the land to be used for construction while the former owner, the aristocrat Lyubov Andreyevna Ranevskaya, takes the path of self-imposed exile in Paris together with her daughter Anya.

Beyond the palimpsestic references that bridge the two plays, Ularu maintains Chekhov's insistence that the characters' ideas must be "examined like objects." But if Chekhov's satiric detachment in *The Cherry Orchard* is often that of the practicing physician who views the human species with a clinical eye, Ularu's serious engagement spotlights in *A Sequel* his characters' internal geography in the ideologically troubled days of a rising Bolshevism. If Chekhov, in the words of one of his most famous characters, Lyubov Ranevskaya, the leading female protagonist of *The Cherry Orchard*, "talks about things that don't matter,"[1] Ularu reveals in his own play

41

an intertext enriched by one of the major characteristics of postmodern theatrical practices: how to rewrite history in a postmodern culture that has dismantled the idea of history mainly through the relativization of the axial events of history in personal experience. In *A Sequel*, the gradual Communist takeover that Chekhov could not have anticipated in *The Cherry Orchard* provides the axial historical event that transfers the dynamic of historical moments onto the personal plane. Thus, in the changing political and social climate that Ularu's play proposes, the exploration of the relation between its characters and the performative present of the Communist takeover foreshadows the central ideology of Bolshevism and of a police-state: Stalinist tactics, Party rhetoric, and aberrant politics disguised as class struggle.

Beyond such recognizable aspects foregrounded in a critical discussion, there is the attraction of Ularu's play as an ideologically and politically constructed ghost text, populated by the ghost of Marxism-Leninism brought to Lyubov Ranevskaya's orchard at the twilight of tsarist Russia. These are, however, not only the ghosts of the dead characters resurrected from Chekhov's original but also the phantasms of an incipient Communism and of the emerging ideological architecture of Stalinism.

The framing device of Ularu's play maintains both the well known topological configuration and the protagonists of *The Cherry Orchard,* several of whom appear as ghosts. The interaction between these fantastic characters and *A Sequel*'s "real" personages weaves a scenic interrelation of literary, artistic, and mental space, a half and half or mezzo-text not only literally but also in terms of life-death. The construction of tone and texture and its antiphonal dialogue resonate with the bittersweet music of ambivalence, of half-real, half-textual occurrences.

More complex than a theatrical *bric-a-brac* or a quaint relic of its great Russian model whose only merit is that of resurrecting ghosts, *A Sequel* also foreshadows a new political and social order in the interrupted patrilineal transmission of social and political authority and in the characters' identity – an "afterlife" instance of dramatic perspectives and political ramifications that are absent from its classical antecedent. Specifically, Ularu's play features pitiable or decrepit characters forced to confront the hollowness of Bolshevik ideology and the political crimes of a brutal, emerging Soviet order, which is itself shrouded in death after the Fall of the Berlin Wall and the demise of Communism in the countries of the former Eastern bloc.

This added perspective that Ularu uses as foundational approach to blur the lines between literary interpretation and historical or political acts enriches the polyvalent integrity of the play's literary discourse through what Joseph Luzzi calls "the rhetoric of anachronism."[2] According to Luzzi, such a device provides a correction against any attempt to reduce the formal matter of literary discourse to the status of mere reflector or mirror of its contextual referents, that is of *A Sequel* as a mere palimpsest of Chekhov's masterpiece; consequently, Ularu's play is both an aesthetic experience and a historically engaged act, allowing the stage performance to explore the representation of history in juxtaposition with personal experience and to become a force-field for transparency and metaphoricity through which to understand the cultural and political context of post-history.

After the watershed triggered by Goethe's review of Alessandro Manzoni's verse drama *Adelchi* (1822)[3] that proclaimed poetic anachronism to be a universal literary category, the notion of anachronism received its most notable treatment in Georg Lukacs's *The Historical Novel*.[4] Here Lukacs writes that the historical novel imbues its protagonists with the "necessary anachronism," by which he means that characters think, feel and behave in a manner that reflects the broad historical and sociopolitical contexts framing their lives.

Moving beyond genre considerations in the category of dramatic representation, Ularu employs in *A Sequel* a rhetoric of anachronism that collapses the boundaries between a literary work's internal means of reference (the characters resurrected from Chekhov's classic play) and its external referential compass made possible by Ularu's post-Communist foreknowledge/awareness of the evils and aberrations of Soviet ideology which *A Sequel* foregrounds in their incipient form. While conforming to the necessary anachronism dictated by Chekhov's original play, the lives and conversations of characters in *A Sequel* also respond to the sophisticated norms of objective progression and historical awareness.

As Ularu's protagonists enter the stage, they maintain their previous lack of moral courage to face their problems and display the same amazing absence of will. Lopakhin, the greedy arrivist, who had purchased Ranevskaya's cherry orchard in Chekhov's play to better his social condition and to liquidate her debts, is now an aging proprietor whose hopes for a better life have failed to materialize. He lives alone, still wallows in his infatuation for Ranevskaya, and continues to hope that she will return to see her aging brother, Gayev, who lives in the old family house with Lopakhin and who goes to the railroad station everyday to be there just in case she happens to return. With them is Dunyasha, Ranevskaya's servant maid who had been impregnated by the caddish Yasha in Chekhov's play. She is now married to Yepikhodov, Lopakhin's rather dull accountant and clerk, who also fancies himself to be a very talented writer and poet and who seems to be unfazed by Dunyasha's infidelities and nagging.

Completing this household and breathing fresh awareness of the past into the present, are the ghosts of Firs, the former serf whose character is a stand-in for the oppressed common man of pre-Communist Russia, and of Grisha, Ranevskaya's son, who had drowned in adolescence during a foolish contest with the son of the local pharmacist, Pyotr (Petya) Trofimov, and who is now a wet ghost. A complementary character to Grisha, not only as a ghost but also for displaying equally foolish boyishness, Firs has been so infantilized by serfdom that he doesn't know how to think. Even as a ghost, Firs is unable to forget his obligations and still worries that Gayev, his old charge, does not dress warmly enough. The pranks of Firs and Grisha light up *A Sequel* and allow the text to transcend the grim reality of a dying world. In Ularu's ingenious revival, Dunyasha's child is said to have almost drowned not because of Yepikhodov's inattention but to allow Grisha, the ghost, to have some fun. The same playful ghosts place pots in the path of Yepihodov, their favorite target, making his gait look clumsy and cumbersome, and thus sealing the perception of the character as dull and slow-witted.

Firs's and Grisha's ludic anachronisms also summon past events and oblige the reader to reminisce the scenes and characters of Chekhov's play. The twosome trigger their own vampiric image by trying to maintain loose control over the house and by playing tricks on its inhabitants, thus suggesting that the past can be very much a feared and tricky presence in the present. In the rhetorical guide that defines the relationship between anachronism and literary practices, these two characters provide a significant measure of what Henri Morier in *Dictionaire de poetique et de rhetorique* calls regressive anachronism or catachronism, i.e., the type of anachronism that does not "update" the past to the present but rather situates the problems of the present in the movements of history.[5] From the ghosts' conversation, we learn of Grisha's father's dissolute life and the excessive spending of the Ranevsky family, especially the eccentric Lyubov Ranevskaya who spends her time and fortune in Paris and neglects the family's land and estate. Such a past still controls the present of *A Sequel* and accounts for the characters' moral and emotional daze, a feeling also commensurate with the confusing political events of the early Bolshevik Russia.

Ranevskaya (Elena Ivanka), Lopakhin (Petre Băcioiu) and Yepikhodov (Ovidiu Crişan) in Nic Ularu's staging of the play *The Cherry Orchard Sequel* at the National Theatre "Lucian Blaga" in Cluj-Napoca

The conflict of *A Sequel* thus centers on the transition period from the old world of landed gentry to the gradual spread of Bolshevism in Russia – an occurrence marked in the play by the confrontation between Lopakhin and Raneskaya on the one hand and Petya Trofimov and Comrade Boris on the other. As these two groups belong to easily discernable political sides of the old, tsarist and the new, Bolshevik Russia, respectively, the character of Yepikhodov suggests the inability of the middle class to comprehend the class struggle and the senseless triviality of a world nostalgic for the past and unable to understand the present. Missing from *A Sequel* is Ranevskaya's beautiful daughter, Anya, whose presence is only felt in the play as a wound or an unaccountable blot or stain on the once elegant Russian gentry: she is said to work as a prostitute in Paris, under the protection of the former servant Yasha, acting as her pimp. Adding to all these characters' lack of a specific gravity as they seem to hold on to their past lives, the ludic ghosts of Firs and Grisha suggest the ineffectual role of the past to avert or impact the Bolshevik Revolution and Stalinist takeover.

The arrival of Trofimov, the young man who had once loved Raneskaya's daughter Anya and who had also benefited from Lopakhin's generous support while being in school, jolts the household from what Petya calls "being stuck in the past"[6] (26) and steers the interpretation of *A Sequel* toward dramatic commentary on the evils of Soviet Communism. A militant Bolshevik and member of the Red Army, Petya is now anxious to gloss over his past attachment to Raneskaya, and especially his once very public infatuation with beautiful Anya. He also needs to prepare the ground for Comrade

47

Boris to receive the "good references" required for the position of cultural propagandist in the region to which Petya aspires to lead politically. As a final gesture of kindness toward his former benefactor, Petya also wants to warn Lopakhin that he needs to leave immediately because he in danger of being deported to Siberia or even executed.

These unmistaken allusions to the monstrous Stalinist tactics, with which Ularu is all-too-familiar after a lifetime spent in Communist Romania, accelerate the spectator's understanding of the past – what must have been the terror of an emerging Bolshevism for the Russian people. Lopakhin's suicide, Ranevskaya's execution-style death and Trofimov's subsequent suicide, all convey in dramatic representation the play's mandate to establish authenticity and veracity by providing an enduring memorial to the tragic events of the traumatic and unforgettable history of a forcibly Stalinized East Central Europe.

By anchoring *A Sequel* into the senseless history of such events so that the spectator can revisit the past, Ularu also constructs his play on a double anachronism: first, his own belated return to Chekhov's play that stands as a pretext or vessel for the dramatic re-creation of an incipient Communism; and second, the anachronism that occurs when the spectator dislodges the time and characters from the play's realm into the present, bringing forth the clash of mentalities, i.e., the brutal reality of an abrupt ideological takeover that transformed political idealism into hatred in Soviet Russia and, as a key effect of literary anachronism, the lingering memory of enforced Stalinism still affecting audiences in East Central Europe.[7]

48

Trofimov (Dan Chiorean) and Comrade Boris (Emanuel Petran) in Nic
Ularu's staging of the play *The Cherry Orchard Sequel* at the National
Theatre "Lucian Blaga" in Cluj-Napoca

Personifying the hideous transformation of revolutionary fervor into senseless cruelty, Petya Trofimov represents the new political order, in which he also recognizes opportunities for his own advancement. His destructive hatred, communicated in such pronouncements as "Lopakhin is dangerous and egotistic...he helped people in order to humiliate them" (28) or in his views of Ranevskaya as someone who "acted like royalty and enjoyed a fortune made by her ancestors with their serf's blood! She and her brother never worked in their lives" (27), bring about the infernal experience of Communism and the suffering of the privileged classes overlooked by history and reduced to silence by the suffocating grip of memory.

In delineated ideological patches, Ularu's play

engages the audience in the activity of digging out linguistic bones and relics not only so that they can be given a proper burial place but also in order to put in perspective old wounds by forcing the flesh open to dig through all the layers of blood and suffering. In *A Sequel*, historical events gush forth from the wounds of Communist history and are legitimized as political truths by the very virtue of their horror. Disseminated throughout the play in traumatic moments of compressed cruelty, dramatic occurrences like the shooting of Ranevskaya by Comrade Boris or the sound of the gunshot that announces Trofimov's suicide when forced to commit murder in the name of Communist principles, function as indices of the time when history explodes; they are also historical signals that encompass the congealed eventfulness of history with which spectators are called to interact. By invoking Comrade Boris's cruelty in shooting an old, ailing woman, *A Sequel* produces an active form of despair that makes spectators aware of history and aware of themselves. Through dramatic complicity, they perform the Benjaminian *"Jetztzeit"* [8] while simultaneously experiencing the horrors of the traumatic Communist era and they also resurrect the ghost of Lenin's fanatic ideology.

It seems as if Ularu's orchard is visited by Lenin's ghost, once again aware that people would never support him and that he must propose a single organ to rule and oversee the creation of Communism: the Party. It is this embarrassing gap between reality (suggested in the old timers of both plays) and aspiration (displayed in the madness of comrade Boris and in Trofimov's feeble attempts to comply) that made Lenin's quasi-religious fidelity to the Party so important and so obligatory – and so haunting in Ularu's *A Sequel* as a political ghost to the improvised peculiar system the Soviet Union and the countries of the Eastern Bloc since the days of the 1945 Yalta agreement had to observe with military discipline and obligatory terror.

The healing ritual Ularu proposes consists of retrieving in the characters' words the pretentious, now ghostly, rhetoric of Soviet ideology. When told that the present times are "shitty," Trofimov brings in the slogans proclaiming that "by simply enrolling in the Communist party people will become happier and healthier"(32). Echoing the fervor of a Bolshevism spearheaded by the tragically deceived figures of culture who championed the Revolution of 1917, Trofimov asserts that "the artist must use his talent to imagine and depict a glorious future …the concerts and theatre performances must take place in factories, in fields, or wherever the workers and peasants need culture. Culture will be in their midst"(30). Such "artistic truths" are as much the laughing stock of today's intellectual as the pranks of Grisha, the wet ghost, are to the audience of Ularu's *Sequel*.

Metamorphosed from ghostly Leninism into political déjà vu, Trofimov's utter nonsense, much like Comrade Boris's destabilizing rhetoric, suggests the regenerative force of aesthetic/dramatic memory that assumes the form of a symbolic resistance to historical and sociopolitical context and triggers the play's gesture of intransigence against the menacing events of neo-Stalinism in the present. For Ularu to speak on behalf of the mind of his characters is akin to any of us speaking on behalf of the dead, for neither the fictional nor the deceased can qualify or edit our words. Yet without this rationally impossible link between the living, the dead, and the imaginary, we cannot have the historical novel or play. Nor can we have memory. When Goethe writes that "all poetry essentially deals in anachronisms,"[9] he grasps the profound and epistemological stakes inherent in the clash of temporalities that inevitably accompanies figurative modes of expression – modes that can not only trick time but also aim to resurrect ghosts and ideology from the dominion of death. Such political ghosts and ideological phantasms as those of *A Sequel* produce knowledge about the past in ways that subvert the more rational and empirical elements traditionally associated with disciplines like history and philosophy.

By contrast with *The Cherry Orchard's* ending, the finale of *A Sequel* underscores this point. In Chekhov's play, as the house is closed down, the characters prepare to follow their various trajectories: Lopakhin to make his fortune; Trofimov to make a better world; Gayev and Ranevskaya to squander their fortune and stifle their opportunities for happiness and fulfillment. In all the planning and worrying, they forget Firs, the loyal retainer, who is locked up and who has no chance of surviving boarded up in the freezing cold. Although condemned to an absurd death, Firs offers a tragic-comic example of a misfortune that rests, like the fate of all the characters in *The Cherry Orchard*, on human caprice and indolence.

The death of comrade Boris in the freezing cold in *A Sequel's* finale, on the other hand, blurs both the dark humor and the larger, dramatic thrust of the play, shifting the characters' concern over what the future holds to the rueful symptoms of Communism and Leninist ideology that offer neither solutions nor remedy – only tragic death in the midst of the cold Russian landscape. Here Dunyasha, looking for Yepikhodov in the snow, one armed with a sickle and the other with a hammer, offers a moment-event whose meaning can be grasped only *post factum*, through the filters of a present that has retained the emblematic sickle and hammer from the statuary group of the worker and the peasant made by the Soviet sculptor Vera Muhina. Arching over the entire Stalinist era to the Soviet Union and Romania, the signature pairing summons Vişniec's lines in *At Table with Marx*, where a sickle and a hammer are not sufficient for the poet-protagonist to "dig a mass grave" for the victims of Communism. The one hundred million faces of the dead seem to hark back in time to the frozen images of Dunyasha and Yepikhodov, surrounded in *A Sequel* by the ghosts of *The Cherry Orchard*.

Notes

1. Chekhov, Anton. *The Cherry Orchard*. Ed. Brian Woolland. Trans. Pam Gems. Cambridge: Cambridge UP, 1996. All quotations are from this edition.

2. Luzzi, Joseph. "The Rhetoric of Anachronism." *Comparative Literature* vol 61, 2009. 69-84.

3. Goethe, Johann Wolfgang von. "Teilnahme Goethes an Manzoni." *Schriften zur Literatur*. Vol. 15. *Werke*. Ed. Ernst Beutler. Zurich: Artemis, 1950. pp 812–43.

4. Lukács, Georg. *The Historical Novel*. Trans. Hannah and Stanley Mitchell. Lincoln: U of Nebraska P, 1970.

5. Morier, Henri. *Dictionnaire de poétique et de rhétorique*. 5th ed. Paris: PUF, 1961.

6. Ularu, Nic. *The Cherry Orchard Sequel*. Cluj-Napoca: Casa Cărții de Știință, 2012. All quotations are from this edition.

7. For a detailed discussion of this type of anachronism, see Greene, Thomas M. "History and Anachronism." *Literature and History: Theoretical Problems and Russian Case Studies*. Ed. Gary Saul Morson. Stanford: Stanford UP, 1986. 205–20.

8. Benjamin, Walter. "The Work of Art in the Age of Mechanical Reproduction." Trans. Harry Zohn. Ed. Hannah Arendt. *Illuminations: Essays and Reflections*. New York: Schocken, 1969. 219-53.

9. Von Goethe, Johann Wolfgang. *Goethes Werke: Vollstandige Ausgabe Letzter Hand*. Vol. 30. Charleston: Nabu Press, 2010.

5. The Fate of A Writer in Stalin's Soviet Union:

Matei Vişniec's *How to Teach the History of Communism to Mental Patients*

In 1935, five years after Mayakovsky's death and the subsequent suppression of his work in the Soviet Union, Stalin propelled him into posthumous fame, in spite of a suspicious suicide, by emphatically praising his legacy. "Mayakovski," decreed Stalin, "was and remains the finest, most talented poet of our Soviet age. Indifference to his memory and his works is a crime."[1]

Stalin, who dominated the world of cinema, literature, and politics and micro-managed the theatre, recognized in Mayakovsky's work an early and important shaper of Soviet culture and consciousness. After all, Mayakovsky had made extraordinary efforts to attach himself to the young Soviet state. In a speech given in Moscow on October 1927, he famously claimed, "I don't give a damn that I am a poet. I'm not a poet, but first and foremost someone who has placed his pen at the service – note, service – of the current moment, the true reality and its guide – the Soviet government and the party."[2]

By praising Mayakovsky, Stalin also wanted to distance himself from Lenin, who disliked the flamboyant poet and playwright. According to Maxim Gorky, who quotes Lenin as saying that "He [Mayakovsky] yells, he makes up these crooked words,"[3] Lenin viewed Mayakovsky with "suspicion and irritation," especially when Mayakovsky resurfaced with new publications, like the narrative poem *150,000,000* (a title indicating the total population of the Soviet Union) at a printing house of the Soviet State. In a note sent to his Minister of Education on May 6, 1921, an irritated Lenin wrote: "Aren't you ashamed to vote for publishing Makyakovsky's *150,000,000* in 5,000 copies? It's nonsense, stupidity, idiotic and pretentious. I think only 1 out of 10 such things should be published and *no more than* 1,500 copies for libraries and eccentrics. And Lunacharsky should be horse-whipped for Futurism."[4]

In spite of Lenin's hostile attitude, the intensity of Mayakovsky's attempt to arouse the people of the young Soviet state could not have been lost on Stalin. Having paralleled in his unique poetry the music of Sergei Prokofiev's "Scythian Suite," Mayakovsky was genuinely inspired by the Bolshevik Revolution, whose beginnings held a very special resonance. In 1917, on October 25 (which became November 7), Mayakovsky was one of the intellectual elite present in the headquarters of the Bolshevik Party at Smolny Palace in Petrograd and watched Lenin at work in establishing the Soviet government. Leaving nothing to be guessed in terms of his political convictions, Mayakovsky, whose allegiances belonged to the group of left art known as Futurist, published the poem "Revolution" as a companion piece to the dramatic overthrow of the old regime in Russia:

> Citizens!
> Today falls the thousand-year "before."
> Today the world's basis is revised.
> Today, to the last coat button
> We will make life over anew.[5]

As he wrote in his autobiography of 1922, Mayakovsky detested everything archaic, everything churchy, and everything Slavonic and proclaimed his Futurism, his atheism and his internationalism as his true pursuits. Mayakovsky's drama, like the Russian Futurists' eccentric outbursts in the early days of the Bolshevik Revolution, was the drama of the young poets, writers, artists, composers, and theatrical figures like Tristan Tzara and the Dadaists, who were scattered throughout East and Central Europe. In an article published in 1914, "We Also Want Meat," Mayakovsky mused about being considered a Futurist.[6] "They say that I am a Futurist," he declares with nonchalance, and then proceeds to define the notion in his own terms:

What is a Futurist? I don't know. I never heard of one. They do not exist.

....

And even the trade name "Futurists" is not ours. Our first books, *A Trap of Judges*, *A Slap in the Face of Public Taste*, *Prayer Book of the Three*, we called simply, collections of a literary group.

It is the newspaper who christened us "Futurists." It's funny! If Vavila were to shout 'Why am I not Evgeny?' what difference would it make?

For us – the young poets – Futurism is the toreador's red cloak, it is needed only for the bulls (poor bulls – I compare them to the critics).

....

In all our manifestoes, in a prominent place on our banners was: "All creativity is free."

Come to us!

We shall receive each of you with dignity…Only keep our language pure of and uneaten up by the phrases of the "venerables."

Today's poetry – is the poetry of strife.

Each word must, like a soldier in the army, be made of meat that is healthy, of meat that is red.

Those who have it – join us!

....

When you tear a car through hundreds of persecuting enemies, there's no point in sentimentalizing: "Oh, a chicken was crushed under the wheels."

Our cruelty has given us strength, so that without having once given into life, we carry our banner: The freedom to create words and to create from words.

Hatred for the language which existed before us.

[The strength] to reject with indignation the wreath of cheap glory made from bathhouse besoms.

[The strength] to stand on the clod of the word WE in a sea of whistles and indignation. [7]

Iconoclastic and innovative, Mayakovsky could not escape the fervor of change brought along by the galloping march toward the revolution and threw his hat in the ring with the Bolsheviks, whose Manifesto demanded "the destruction of privileges and control in the areas of art." Bringing the political and artistic struggle together, Mayakovsky proclaimed, in his unmistakably flamboyant style, that "The Party is a Leninist tank in which we shall out-dis-tance the future!"[8] He also emphasized the need to show grim cruelty toward those unwilling to go along with the violent changes bathed in "the toreador's red cloak."

Mayakovsky's work, which was assumed to be simply harnessed to move the ideological machinery of the Soviet State, became problematic at best after being abruptly interrupted by his suicide in 1930. What, one may ask, if Mayakovsky had lived? Would he have become another Sholokhov? Or would he have suffered the fate of Mayakovsky's protagonists in the play *The Bathhouse* who ends up rejected and cast out of a time machine? The final scene of this play, in which the protagonist is left to wonder publicly if such rejection means "that I and my like are not needed for Communism,"[9] sounds the note of despair of an individual left out of the Communist project. More and more such a project is beginning to resemble a hardening scientific utopia that threatens to crash not only its protagonist but also the playwright.

A similar disenchantment with the Soviet state resonates earlier in *The Bedbug*, a play announced in the Prologue as "a politico-futurological blast/ which invents a satiric future out of a that false dawn/The comically deluded time, just after the Revolution/In Russia, and just before Stalin's terror."[10] Using his "Futuristic pen to skewer many hearts [and] to drive a sharpened stake through what he calls Socialist-Realistic, fear-beshitted 'art'" (3), Mayakovsky mounts a momentous attack on the Soviet utopia through the words of the Mechanic, a character in the play who summarizes the failed project of political transformation:

> The Road toward Utopia is paved with Blood
> And Stone
> There's many with me Comrades,
> I know I'm not Alone
> The Godless Party promises
> A Heaven for our Eyes
> But Who will Pay for This?
> We're paying with our Lives –

We're Building a Road to a better World
For Night on Seven Years,
But now the Mists have moved away,
To show the Path we steered.
The Road to Utopia leads straight to a Wall
And our work was in Vain,
'Cos the Wall don't want Us,
The Wall don't want Us
The Wall don't want Us at All. (17-18)

Having been preserved in a gigantic frozen ice cube, the play's protagonist, Ivan Varlet, is resurrected fifty years later to find futuristic city streets, with futuristic pedestrians, and a new Soviet Union where "it is irrational to end life before it stops being of use to the Party" (30). Varlet's regret for the old times, which is coupled with his lament for the present Soviet society that appears as a merely failed project, results in the play's binary image of the early Bolshevik times and the new workers' state. Far from suggesting a linearity of purpose and societal transformation, the new Soviet order triggers Varlet's chant "The Loveboat Has Crushed," whose lines echo the Prologue and may well be reflective of Mayakovsky's own prescient resentment:

This is why I would rather Die
What did we fight for in the Good Old Days
Memory's in short Supply
Censored and sanitized
All the Chips were stacked on Red
We took our chances with the Gun
We Danced and Sang, we thought we'd won
What Happened/
Why did we let it Go
Sweet Proletariat

A Beautiful Plan, the Perfection of Man-
I would have died for That

I would have died for That
Now we're all out of Time
We were afloat on Dreams
But the Loveboat has Crashed. (41)

Even though Varlet has not been cured of his prior drinking and depravity during the fifty years spent in the ice cube and ends up being displayed in a cage at the zoo as the object of contempt and disapproval, his cry "Look, you don't want me here" (41) echoes once again the despair of an individual as a possible alter-ego of Mayakovsky, isolated and disenchanted with the Bolshevik utopia. The early death of Velimir (Viktor) Hlebnikov (1885-1922) and tragic fate of Nikolay Gumiliev (1886-1921), who had championed the Bolsheviks' cause only to be executed in the earlier days of the Communist takeover, could not have failed to play a role in Mayakovsky's growing disappointment with an incipient Stalinism and the dogmatic limits which Bosheviks placed upon the Soviet intellectual life.

Such a nascent disappointment surrounding Mayakovsky's situation begs for a similar type of argument as the one Georg Lukacs formulates in the case of the troubled hero who finds that "the outside world is no longer adapted to the individual's ideas and the ideas become subjective facts-ideals-in his soul."[11] According to Lukacs, when this ideal destroys the organic unity between character and world, the character finds himself in opposition to the world, a rebellious activity that would have made Mayakovsky a prime candidate for political dissent, and a sure victim, in Stalin's Soviet Union.

Chances are slim that Mayakovsky would have survived the Great Terror of 1936-1939 when at least six hundred published authors, almost a third of the members of the Union of Soviet Writers, were arrested; or the imprisonment and execution of the OBERIU members who called themselves "a leftist group of revolutionary art" (Igor Terentiev in 1937, and Aleksandr Vvedensky and Daniel Harms and in 1941 and 1942, respectively), the torture and executions of Isaac Babel and Vsevolod Meyerhold, or a likely deportation to the Gulag. Had he escaped such death sentences, Mayakovsky might have ended up in a mental institution, which was another effective way by which Stalin disposed of problematic intellectuals and writers.

In this context, Matei Vişniec's *How to Teach the History of Communism to Mental Patients*, a play "dedicated to Daniel Harms and to all writers who have died in the jails of tyrants," offers a plausible alternative to the conditions in which Mayakovsky would have spent the remaining days of his life in the totalitarian Soviet state. His fate may well have been that of Yuri Petrovski, the writer protagonist of Vişniec's play, who is portrayed as an honest and decent person, with a fine sense of irony and justice, a compassionate heart, and a tragic destiny.

First performed at the Open Fist Theatre Company, Hollywood, in April 2000, Vişniec's play was originally written in French, *L'histoire du Communisme racontée aux malades mentaux*, and published by Editions LANSMAN, Belgium in that same year. The English translation, in the version of Jeremy Lawrence and Catherine Popesco, which is extensively quoted here, exists only as a manuscript and has been used in various adaptations of the play for stagings in the United States, Romania, and France.

Like Solzhenitsyn, who was himself a casualty of Stalinism and who wrote relentlessly about Soviet life in works like *The First Circle* and *Cancer Ward* because he was determined to make a full and detailed disclosure of the truth about Stalin and Stalinism, Vişniec too had been robbed of his youth and personal freedom in Stalinist Romania and had to take the path of exile in 1987, when he asked for political exile in France and began to write against Stalin's and Communism's all-pervasive lies. For both writers Stalin is a powerful emblem of cruelty and a sinister symbol of a way of life and system of beliefs. Solzhenitsyn's *The First Circle* sketches a portrait of Stalin as a monstrous creation of the propaganda machine, an aging man who sits alone at night reading his official biography and trying to convince himself of the identity which was invented for him there:

> This man's name filled the world's newspapers, was uttered by thou- sands of announcers in hundreds of languages... It had been given to a multitude of cities and squares, streets and boulevards... and a group of Moscow journalists had proposed that it be given also to the Volga and to the moon. And he was only a little old man with a desiccated double chin which was never shown in his portraits. (86)[12]

Solzhenitsyn's portrayal of Stalin and the state organs anticipates with remarkable clarity Michel Foucault's description of state power. Speaking of the minutiae involved in the creation of a prison system, Foucault writes about "Small acts of cunning endowed with a great power of diffusion; ... attentive 'malevolence' that turns everything to account. Dis-cipline is a political anatomy of detail."[13]

In describing the finer points of the Soviet arrest routine at the Mavrino Institute, a fancy name for the extended Moscow prison that housed some of the state's leading scientists, linguists, and artists, Solzhenitsyn makes explicit the morally devastating effect of that attention to detail aimed to break down the detainees' strength of character:

> Each time, and always for a different reason, they asked him to do something that seemed inconsequential compared with the major battle that lay ahead-and each time it seemed not worth being stubborn about something so trivial. But the total effect of this procedure was to break the prisoner's will completely. (532)

The portrait of Stalin in *The First Circle* depicts a man who is obsessed with bringing everything under his control, no matter how small or apparently insignificant. Yet it is precisely this attitude, Solzhenitsyn argues, which has destroyed Russia. By creating an apparatus of terror and control which could include any thought, any opinion, any deed done or undone and which considered each citizen a potential "traitor to the state," Stalin had destroyed the will of his own nation to act, lest it act incorrectly.

But if both Solzhenitsyn and Foucault agree that force applied with attention to the minute particulars can make a prison house of the whole society, Vişniec goes one step further and structures his play on the political space of a mental institution which serves as a microcosm of the entire Soviet Union, and where Stalin himself is imprisoned. In *History of Communism*, Stalin's image is caught in an informational loop, a distillation of elements combined in the shadow of an evil power where the "Man of Steel" is facing his own mortality after having destroyed the lives of millions of Soviet citizens through vicious caprice, paranoia, and inhumanity.

The opening of Vișniec's *How to Teach the History of Communism to Mental Patients* in Mona Chirilă's staging of the play at the National Theatre "Lucian Blaga" in Cluj-Napoca

Vișniec's play opens with the arrival of the writer Yuri Petrovski at Moscow's Central Hospital for Mental Disorders, where he has been dispatched for the stated purpose of teaching Marxist Leninist and Stalinist ideology to the patients. As in Zamyatin's *We*, a satire in which the Soviet State is a space where love "has long since been forgotten," in the mental hospital of *History of Communism* there is no accommodating space for the assertion of the patients', or Yuri Petrovski's, individual self. As Yuri Petrovski quickly realizes, the tragedy of their lives is a remote cry from the notes of self-love which Mayakovsky lavishes on himself in early plays like *Vladimir Mayakovski, A Tragedy*. More to the point, Vişniec's play resonates with Yuri Petrovski's tragic fate as a possible dramatic sequel to Mayakovsky's own muffled cry for help in *The Bathhouse* and *The Bedbug*. Mixing tears with uncontrollable fits, the patients of the mental hospital move along walls that stand for jail cells, and their outbursts give a shift of dramatic perspective at crucial moments, as the hospital director, Grigori Dekanozov, moves them around like he would chess pieces, taking them from one extreme of mental darkness and dispossession to another. In foregrounding the mental hospital and its patients, the writer Yuri Petrovski, and the hospital administrators, Vişniec's play functions as an extreme example of a state's use of force through direct institutional and psychological control.

It may be interesting to add that such institutions of the Soviet Union's system of *psikhushkas*, or psychiatric prison wards used as "reeducation" centers to bring dissident intellectuals back in line by means of chemical straight jackets, were anticipated in Samuel Beckett's play *What Where*[14]. This short piece, which Beckett called a "dramaticule," offers as its central structure the interrogation chamber and focuses on the senselessness of torture, the punishment which the characters inflict upon each other to find out *what* happened and *where*.

Adding a torturous testimonial to Beckett's fictional inquisitors, Bam, Bem, Bim and Bom, whose bell-like names echo a death knell, the dissident mathematician, Leonid Plyusch, who was imprisoned in a series of such hospitals before he was allowed to leave Russia through the intercession of Amnesty International, describes "treatment" at the Dnipropetrovsk hospital:

> I could see the effects of the potent sedative haloperidol on my fellow inmates and wondered why drugs were administrated in quarantine. One inmate was writhing in convulsions, head twisted to the side of eyes bulging. Another patient was gasping for breadth and his tongue was lolling. A third was screaming for the nurse and begging for a corrective to alleviate the physical effects of haloperidol. The drug was given in such large doses in order to reveal the malingerers and to break any resistance. The very first day a criminal who had been simulating amnesia, gave us and went to see Kamenetskaya (the psychiatrist) to confess. (*History's Carnival*, 305.) [15]

Bringing the actuality of Stalin's mental institutions into his play, Vişniec relies on real people like Plyusch who were destroyed. This is the case of Maria Spiridonova, the dedicated Bolshevik who had served as the head of the Socialist Revolutionary party until February 1919 and who appears as a patient in *History of Communism*. In December,

1918, Maria Spiridonova had vigorously condemned the daily terror practiced by the Cheka, the name of the secret police during this period. Shortly thereafter, she was arrested in February 1919 and condemned by the Revolutionary Tribunal to "Detention in a Sanatorium given her hysterical condition". Her case was the first internment of a political dissident in a mental hospital during the Soviet regime and her presence in the play adds the testimonial of truth to the dramatic production.

Having lost everything and doomed to life imprisonment, the patients in Vişniec's play are understood to be enemies of the state, whose guilt has been established, as in the case of Maria Spiridonova, through mysterious verdicts. Several weeks before Stalin's death in 1953, they lead a life of horror that conjures the almost surreal cycle of suffering in the Soviet Union. The hospital supervisors, Grigori Dekanozov (Director of the Hospital), Stepan Rozanov (Assistant Director of the Hospital) and Katia Ezova (Medical Assistant of the Hospital), seem to blend with their patients into an amorphous mass, much in the same way as the patients and the hospital personnel converge as a collectively sick body in Solzhenitsyn's *Cancer Ward*, so that the entire population of the hospital, although carefully differentiated, is a static collage that stunts the characters' growth and development – and thus persuasively evokes life in an oppressive system for both victims and victimizers.

Dekanozov (Dragoş Pop) and a terrified Katia Ezova (Eva Crişan) in
Vişniec's *How to Teach the History of Communism to Mental Patients* in
Mona Chirilă's staging of the play at the National Theatre "Lucian Blaga" in
Cluj-Napoca

Indeed, by presenting his characters within an amalgamated body, Vişniec suggests that the difference between the patients and the hospital administrators is largely illusory – everyone is in the same trap, or "shit," as Yuri Petrovski states in not so veiled terms. No less trapped into this web of artificial ideology and lies is

Stalin himself, who is dramatized as an ailing character, no longer feeding on adulatory phrases, fearful and haunted by the ghosts of his neglected second wife, Nadezhda Alliluyeva, and of his own mother, mentally weak and withering in the face of fast approaching death and suggesting that the unifying force of *History of Communism* is the shadow of death.

Like Solzhenitsyn's novel, Vişniec's play is restricted in time and space, as the absurd but fully plausible events unfolding in the hospital's close quarters suggest the Soviet Union's world of camps, prisons, and hospital wards. The opening of the play features the mental hospital's choir, which suggests from the start the collective experience of the Soviet people, producing the effect of a microcosm. Acting as the conductor of the Choir, Katia Ezova leads everyone in singing "The Song of the Partisans" while Timofei, one of the patients, dries a tear. Since most of the patients, unlike Timofei, cannot even wipe their own tears because they are in straight jackets, it is understood not only that he is a favorite, but also that the only freedom left at all is to be permitted to cry. In the sinister mockery that pervades the play, the cherished solidarity of the hospital space translates into having Timotei dry the tears of his straight-jacketed comrades.

The absurdity that characterizes life in the Soviet Union devolves into the play's improbability and unleashed harrowing terror. In his office, and moments later when he introduces Yuri Petrovski, the Hospital Director speaks about the victorious transformation of Man in Socialism, following the instructions of "Great Lenin" and "Mighty Stalin." The need to have a great writer like Yuri Petrovski sent to the mental hospital to teach and model the patients in the greatness of Soviet ideology mocks Stalin's much quoted invitation that the writers be "engineers of human soul" and brings it to a rousing satire in Grigori Dekanozov's plea to a terrified and disoriented Yuri Petrovski:

> Comrade Yuri Petrovski, you must write stories to tell the history of Communism to our mental patients ... Use your talent to tell us in simple words the history of Communism and the Great October Socialist Revolution. Use your talent so that the mentally ill can also have access to the light of the Workers' Movement. Use your talent and your patriotism so the mentally ill may feed on the hope that the Great October Socialist Revolution has brought to all the workers of all the countries in the whole wide world. I know, dear comrade Yuri Petrovski, that you are going to find the words that go straight to the hearts of our mental patients. Our initial sessions on the beauty of Art and Literature will be held twice a week. All the mental patients of our institution: the slightly, moderately or deeply debilitated, those suffering from schizophrenia, autism, or depression, neurotics of all sorts will be invited to listen to you bi-weekly. All of them. Except perhaps, those in high security. We'll come up with something else for them. That is to say, we'll have specially organized sessions just for them.

Created in 1932 to destroy talent and creativity that did not serve the dictates of Socialist Realism, the Soviet Writers' Union had been the object of satire in the isolated case of works like Bulgakov's *The Master and Margarita*. Bulgakov's play *The Crimson Island* is a humorous portrayal of the Soviet theatre world's kowtowing to Stalinist censorship as an effective instrument of totalitarian oppression and fear. In the play's thinly-disguised parody, the theatre director takes the impositions of the Party ideologue Savva Lukich even further than the dictates of the Central Repertory Committee which Bulgakov was lampooning. To incur favor with the Party designated censor, the theatre director alters the play's finale by having British soldiers join a tropical island's natives in celebrating the victory of their own Revolution and waving red flags.

Dekanozov (Dragoş Pop) and Yuri Petrovski (Cristian Rigman) in Vişniec's *How to Teach the History of Communism to Mental Patients* in Mona Chirilă's staging of the play at the National Theatre "Lucian Blaga" in Cluj-Napoca

In reminding Yuri Petrovski his duties to instruct the patients by focusing on the final argument, "That is why the Writers Union has sent you to us," Vişniec's Grigori

Dekanozov confines not only the play's individual writer, but through extension the entire organization of Soviet writers to the narrow channel of mental blackouts that destroy the very people who should be fighting against totalitarianism. Fulfilling the Party-mandated mission, Soviet writers become tools of the Stalinist propaganda machine who, in the words of the mildly mentally debilitated Timotei, "are sent everywhere: to the workers, to the peasants, to the soldiers, to get things going."

After ridiculing the whole idea of a writer's mission in the Soviet Union, Vişniec's play engages Yuri Petrovski on a bitter tour of moral exploration. A man of robust mental health and freedom from neurosis, Yuri Petrovski seems determined to make a full disclosure of the truth about Soviet life. He is genuinely horrified by the absurd deification of Stalin in Katia Ezova's poem, which she recites for him, and he courageously denounces the practice of having those who did not want to see things through with Stalin's eyes sent to Siberia, to the Gulag.

Yuri Petrovski seems particularly keen on the definition of Utopia as "being in deep shit and wanting to get out," an allusion to the Soviet Union's conceit in calling itself a scientific utopia and a courageous exposure of the absurd rationalizations that justify the glaring injustices of Communist practices. One of the pathetic characters in mental hospital is Ivan Mikadoi Gamarovski, a caricature of the Soviet man whose declamations about the achievements of his past fifteen years in the institution humorously show Vişniec's intention to portray the hospital as a parodic allegory of the Soviet Union. "We created the free zone ten years ago," declares Gamarovski comically unaware of the dislocation of the social order, "we have here a circle of revolutionary studies, a casino, a tribunal that works 24 hours a day, the People-Who-Met-Stalin Club." For Vişniec, as for Solzhenitsyn, the most powerful weapon is irony, deft and never gentle, used to make sarcastic sport of the Soviet vocabulary and rationalizations in this political fantasy that examines the crushed human condition of the mental patients.

One of the finest characters in the play is Katia Ezova, who seems to subsist on a disarming ingenuity. She writes poetry, about thirty poems about frogs and tears, that provide a refuge for her wasted life, and she does not appear to be hypocritical in her devotion to Stalinist idealism, conveyed in lines that denote the steady diet of propaganda:

> Stalin: you are our light
> In the night without end
> Stalin you caress
> and possess every thought that we send.
>
> Stalin you are our reason to be
> Stalin in us you live eternally
> Stalin all we have is thanks to you
> Stay Stalin stay, we will make your dream come true

When making love to Yuri Petrovski, Katia looks like a haunted animal; later on, her interrogation and the insults she has to endure for her alleged sexual depravity allude to the routine traffic in questionnaires and dossiers, the constant surveillance and the threat of having one's life examined with brutality by demented Soviet bureaucrats like Dekanozov. His accusations, "You know you are a filthy whore, Katia Ezova," escalate to the most acid indictment of the Soviet sure-fire formulae. "We can never build the new society, the new man, the radiant future of the working class," a furious Dekanozov screams at the terrified Katia, "with filthy whores who fuck the deeply debilitated."

Katia's tearful confession that she has slept with the writer Gamarovski brings into focus the depth of cultural and political references in Vişniec's play. In presenting on stage Timofei's stated acceptance of Yuri Petrovski in the mental hospital ("You're one of us now"), and the extended invitation for Yuri Petrovski to attend the writer Gamarovski's fifteenth anniversary as a patient, the play becomes a strong polemic of the political norms and operative standards of Soviet literature. At the party meeting in "Solitary," a word which echoes the dreaded confinement reserved to the disobedient detainees of Stalin's jails and deportation camps, Gamarovski's appointment of Yuri Petrovski to the position of "Commissioner of Literature in our provisional government" marks the play's shift toward its central topic: in the tormented world of the Soviet Union writers are mere political tools of a vast propaganda machine, often assessing the world, as in Solzhenitsyn's case, in the confinement of prisons, camps, and hospital wards.

The corrosive atmosphere of terror, fear and suspicion frayed the fabric of culture and fatally poisoned the moral climate of Stalin's Russia while the West maintained an ambivalent wonder, particularly regarding the fate of the Soviet writers and artists. As their Soviet colleagues were blamed for participating in "conspiratorial terrorist organization" and for being agents of foreign intelligence services out to destroy the Soviet Union, writers like Henry Barbusse, whose book the patient Timotei gives as a gift to Yuri Petrovski, continued to praise Stalin and exalt the Soviet State. In the half-contemptuous, half-pitying dramatic moment of the scene, the audience is left to wonder which of Barbusse's books Timotei has picked for Yuri Petrovski to read – the 1928 book about the marvel that was Georgia or the 1935 official biography of Stalin, both of which are sarcastically included in Vişniec's "Key to Historical Names and References" listed at the end of *History of Communism*.

The accusations Stalin made against the Soviet writers, who were subsequently summarily tried, and then were imprisoned and repeatedly tortured and interrogated, were the immediate a result of their contacts with Andre Gide during the French Communist writer's visit in Moscow to speak on behalf of the Association of Writers in Defense of Culture that was headed by Malraux. Stalin's fears that these exchanges with the West could be problematic for the Soviet Union materialized when Gide, who had appeared to be delighted by everything while in Moscow, condemned everything he had seen just as vehemently once he was back in Paris in his book *Return from Russia* (*Au retour de L'USSR*), which came out in 1936. One wonders why Gide had been so enthusiastic in the first place since the last days in his sojourn in the USSR coincided with the open Moscow trial of the "anti-Soviet united center" (the old Bolsheviks who were opposed to Stalin) and their execution two months after Gorky's death in 1936.

Gide's change of attitude toward the Soviet Union was perceived by Stalin as an act of sabotage, a calculated move to discredit the USSR. Declaring both Gide and Malraux to be spies and saboteurs, and intent on sending a terrifying message to the Russian intellectual elite, Stalin ordered the arrest of many Soviet writers, such as Isaac Babel and the theatre director Vsevolod Meyerhold, who were declared "traitors to the state" for having been in contact with the two French writers.

Stalin's insistence on the ties that Babel and Meyerhold had forged with the French had its own relevance vis-à-vis the international scene. Specifically, such accusations for spying on behalf of the French powers could be used in the international arena against any public suspicion that might have been raised about the advisability of the impending Hitler-Stalin Pact, the infamous German-Soviet Non-Aggression Pact signed by Ribbentrop (Hitler's minister) and Molotov, Stalin's most faithful servant and Commissioner of the People for Foreign Affairs. Stalin's perverse manipulation of the Soviet Union's foreign policy by proving such vigilant unmasking of the spying in order to validate the need to sign a pact with Hitler, becomes quite transparent in *History of Communism*. In the play's dramatic intricacies, the mental hospital's patient identified as The Stranger (*L'Étranger*), who uncontrollably calls out "Ribbentrop-Molotov," echoes Stalin's murderous tactics and unmasks the dictator's evil agenda.

By dramatizing the tragic fate of the fictional writer Yuri Petrovski, the play *History of Communism* offers a moving enactment of and testimony to the crimes of the Stalinist social and political forces unleashed in the aftermath of the Soviet writers' engagement with the Association of Writers in the Defense of Culture that was headed by Malraux. In unmasking the mental hospital as a type of Stalinist "machine like no other," to quote the opening of Kafka's *In the Penal Colony*, that is a machine for killing that worked perfectly and whose purpose was to maintain normal appearances, Vişniec's *History of Communism* delivers a harrowing account of the murders and executions of the Great Terror that sucked the Soviet writers into the funnel of Stalin's repressions. Through the art of theatrical representation and politically subversive dramatization, Vişniec brings to the stage the grotesque and terrifying dimensions of the Stalinist criminal terror and the tragic fate of writers in the Soviet Union. In the decade that began with Mayakovsky's suicide, they were left to write under the dictates of mental hospital directors like Grigory Dekanozov, who in Vişniec's play greets the arrival of Yuri Petrovski by stating, "I am convinced, comrade, that certain mental disorders can be cured by hearing a clear, concise and compelling narration of the History of Communism. Long Live Mighty Stalin!"

Compressed and crowded, the mental hospital in Vişniec's play is a space of confinement that embodies the spirit of evil; it also produces the effect of a microcosm which replaces the artificial hierarchies of the outside world with a similar scale meant to suggest that everyone is essentially in the same trap. The close interaction of administrators and patients with diverse social, political, cultural, and even ethnic backgrounds brings ironic contrasts and reveals Communism's all-pervasive lies and the anxiety and terror that covered the whole country. The source of evil is the demented Stalinist system, with its poisonous ideology, its perpetration and deification of the lie, and its compulsion to waste and destroy human life.

With a meticulous portrait gallery of characters, complete with their central experiences and entangled personal relationships, *History of Communism* generates a site for imaginary identification with Stalinism by projecting for the spectators an imagined identification of the Soviet Union with Romania, a nation that was also shaped by Communism. The relationship of the nation to its own history and to itself ultimately is always about the relationship among the people themselves, and is the secret behind every attempt to cope with memory and the past. Thus Vişniec's contemporaries must find the courage to probe deeply into the complicated and frequently paradoxical relationship between the stage and one's own emotional engagement with the Stalinist era in post-Communism.

Katya Ezova's hysterical outburst at the announcement of Stalin's death ("Stalin, you are with us, in us...We owe you everything, we owe you everything, Stay with us, stay with us") and the final scene of the play featuring Stalin's death as a mere departure ("Stalin turns his head and looks at the patients in a serene and generous fatherly way") are a strong indication that the play is not dedicated to retrospectively get even with Communist totalitarianism by unmasking its terror and evil practices. Its intention is to prevent the memory of quotidian culture from romanticizing the past (of the state that perished with Communism) and from allowing it to fall into oblivion in two ways. On an immediate level, *History of Communism* provides a space for information exchange and promotes an understanding of the history, the living nightmare, and the suffering of all people under Communism. On a political plane, the play is all about the future, about an active engagement in the process of the post-Communist transition. Since oblivion can overshadow memory and produce deep fissions between generations and political convictions, a society that desires a better future must not forget the past; on the contrary, it needs to assess and learn from the lived experiences of the past, and thus be mindful of the history of Communism before directing its gaze to the future.

Notes

1. A.D.P. Briggs, *Vladimir Mayakovski: A Tragedy*. Oxford: Willem A. Meeuws, 1979. 121-22.

2. Quoted in R. Rudnitskii, Rezhisser Meierkhol'd [Meyerhold the Director] Moscow 1969, 237.

3. Volkov, Solomon. *The Magical Chorus: A History of Russian Culture from Tolstoy to Solzhenitsyn*. Trans. Antonina W. Bouis. New York: Alfred Knopf, 2008. 67.

4. Ibid. 67. Lenin's words are also quoted in Tom Stoppard's *Travesties*, a play that features Lenin, alongside James Joyce and Tristan Tzara, as one of the shapers of the twentieth-century culture.

5. Published in *Novaja zhjsn*, 29, Petrograd, 1917.

6. This article was published in the newspaper *Nov'*, No. 116 Moscow, Nov. 16, 1914.

7. Some of the last paragraphs are modified quotations from *A Slap in the Face of Public Taste*, signed by Mayakovsky, Burliuk, Kruchenykh, and Khlebnikov. The entire fragment is from *The Ardis Anthology of Russian Futurism*, ed. Ellendea Proffer and Carl R. Proffer, Dexter: Lakeland Press, 1980, 187-189.

8. See http://vlmayakovsky.narod.ru/annenkov_5.html, Ju. Annenkov, *Dnevnik moich vstrech. Vladimir Mayakovsky.*

9. Mayakovsky, Vladimir. *Plays*. European Drama Classics. Evanston: Northwestern University Press.1995. 332-335. All quotations from *The Bathhouse* are from this edition.

10. Mayakovsky, Vladimir. *The Bedbug and Selected Poetry*. Bloomington: Indiana University Press. 1975. 2. All quotations from *The Bedbug* are from this edition.

11. *A Historico-Philosophical Essay on the Form of Great Epic Literature* trans. Anna Bostock . Cambridge: MIT Press, 1971. 78.

12. *The First Circle* trans. Thomas P. Whitney. New York: Harper,

1968. All quotations are from this edition.

13. Michel Foucault, "Docile Bodies," *The Foucault Reader*. Ed. Paul Rabinow. New York: Pantheon, 1984.183.

14. Written for the Graz theatre festival, Beckett's *What Where* premiered on 15 June, 1983, the same day as *Catastrophe*, a similar piece that Beckett wrote in honor of the then-jailed Czech dramatist Vaclav Havel. In both plays, politics is not an abstraction; rather, it is experienced as personal pain, derived from the dramatist's apprehension of human suffering.

15. Plyusch, Leonid. *History's Carnival: A Dissident's Autobiography*. Ed.and trans. Marco Carynnyk. New York and London: Harcourt, Brace Jovanovich, 1979.

6. About the Authors

VLAD ZOGRAFI

Vlad Zografi was born in Bucharest, Romania in 1960. He graduated from the Faculty of Physics at the University of Bucharest and, after obtaining a scholarship in France, was awarded a Ph.D. in atomic physics from the University of Paris-Sud, Orsay. He published several articles in international specialty journals.

In 1990, after his literary debut with a story in the prestigious *România literară* literary journal, he published a volume of stories, *Genunchiul stîng sau genunchiul drept* (The Left Knee or the Right Knee, Eminescu Press, 1993) and a novel *Omul nou* (The New Man, Albatros Press, 1994). His next publications included several volumes of plays *Isabela, dragostea mea* (Isabela, Mon Amour, Unitext Press, 1997); *Oedip la Delphi* (Oedipus at Delphi, Humanitas Press, 1997); *Regele și cadavrul* (The King and the Corpse, Editura All, 1998); *Viitorul e maculatură* (The Future is Waste, Humanitas Press, 1999); *Petru* (Peter or The Sun Spots, Humanitas Press, 2007); *America și acustica* (America and Acoustics, Humanitas Press, 2007); *Toate mințile tale* (All Your Minds, Humanitas Press, 2011).

Three of these books, *Isabela, dragostea mea*, *Viitorul e maculatură* and *America și acustica* were awarded special prizes by Romania's Writers' Union. The plays *Petru*, *Regele și cadavrul* (The King and the Corpse), *Orgasm* (Orgasm), *Viitorul e maculatură* (The Future is Waste), *Creierul* (The Brain), *Atelier* (Workshop) were staged in România, Germany, Sweden, Italy, France and Hungary. Zografi's book, *Kiss Me: Confessions of a Bare-Footed Leper*, a collection of plays and critical essays, was published in the United States (Bettie Youngs Book Publishers, Gardena: California, 2011).

Zografi also translated in Romanian (with Vlad Russo) the complete plays of Eugène Ionesco.

NIC ULARU

Nic Ularu is the recipient of the OBIE award for outstanding achievement in Off-Broadway theater in New York (2003) and has extensive playwright and director credits in USA and Europe, including theatres in Sweden, Northern Ireland and Romania.

His recent freelance work as playwright and director includes several acclaimed productions at LaMaMa - New York, Teatrul Foarte Mic, Bucharest - Romania, "O" Teatret - Sweden, National Theatre of Constanta - Romania, and National Theatre of Cluj - Romania.

Nic Ularu's play *Cherry Orchard Sequel* produced at LaMaMa got the New York Times theatre critics pick in 2008. Since 2009, Ularu directed the play at the National Theatre of Cluj – Romania. *The Cherry Orchard Sequel* is in the theatre repertory since its acclaimed opening. *Cherry Orchard Sequel* was also translated in Polish and Russian.

Another play, *The System*, written and directed by Nic Ularu was produced at LaMaMa and also staged at the International Theatre Festival of Sibiu, Romania and the National Theatre of Constanta, Romania.

In addition to his national and international playwright / director activity Nic Ularu is a scenographer. His designs appeared in the USA national entries at the Prague Quadrennial International Exhibitions of scenography in 2007, 2003 and 1998. In 2005 Ularu co-designed the exhibit and designed the poster of the World Stage Design Exhibition, Toronto – Canada. He was appointed by United States Institute of Theatre

Technology as the leading designer and curator of the USA National Exhibit at the Prague Quadrennial International Exhibition of 2007.

Nic Ularu is Professor of Theatre at the University of South Carolina, Columbia, USA.

MATÉI VIŞNIEC

Matéi Vişniec was born in Romania in 1956. From an early age, he discovered literature as a space dedicated to freedom. He draws his strengths from Kafka, Dostoevsky, Poe, Lautréamont. He loves the Surrealists, the Dadaists, absurd and grotesque theatre, surrealist poetry, fantastic literature, magical realism, even the realist Anglo-Saxon theatre. He loves everything except Socialist Realism.

Vişniec studied philosophy at Bucharest University and became an active member of the so-called Eighties Generation, who left a clear stamp on the Romanian literature. He believes in cultural resistance, and in literature's capacity to demolish totalitarianism. Above all, Matéi Vişniec believes that theatre and poetry can denounce manipulation through "great ideas", as well as brainwashing through ideology.

Before 1987 Matéi Vişniec had made a name for himself in Romania by his clear, lucid, bitter poetry. Starting with 1977, he wrote drama; the plays were much circulated in the literary circles but were barred from staging. In September 1987, Vişniec left Romania for France, where he was granted political asylum. He started writing in French and began working for *Radio France Internationale*. At the present time, Vişniec has had many of his works staged in France, and some twenty of his plays written in French are published (Actes Sud-Papier, L'Harmattan, Lansman). His plays have been staged in more than 30 countries. In Romania, after the fall of

Communism, Matéi Vişniec has become one of the most frequently performed authors.

The work of Matéi Vişniec has been staged in London – **"The Body of a Woman as a Battlefield in the Bosnian War"** at the Young Vic Theatre, in November 2000 and **"The Story of the Panda Bears told by a Saxophonist who has a Girlfriend in Frankfurt"** at the Edinburgh Festival, in August 2005) by Rouge28 Theatre, London.

In the Unites States, the work of Matéi Vişniec has been represented in New York, Chicago, New Jersey, Hollywood and Phoenix.

"How to explain the History of Communism to mental Patients" was first produced in March 2000 at The Open Fist Theatre Company, Hollywood, directed by Florinel Fatulescu and in October 2004 by the Wing & Groove Theatre Company, directed by Bryan White, at the Chopin Theatre in Chicago during the "Playing French" Festival.

"The Chekhov Machine" was produced in February 2005 at The Open Fist Theatre Company, directed by Florinel Fatulescu.

"Paparazzi or Chronicle of an aborted Sunrise" had a public reading at the Actor's Studio in New York, in March 2005, directed by Cosmin Chivu.

"Old Clown wanted" was produced by The New Jersey Repertory Company, in July 2004, directed by Gregory Fortner and in Phoenix at the Arizona State University.

"The Body of Woman as a Battlefield in the Bosnian War" had a public reading at the Steppenwolf Theatre in Chicago, October 2005, during the "Playing French"

Festival, and was staged in Phoenix at the Arizona State University.

"How to Teach the History of Communism to Mental Patients" was produced in Phoenix at the Arizona State University (USA) and at the Theatre Denis, in Hyeres, France.

The company Trap Door Theater from Chicago produced three plays by Matei Vişniec: **"Old clown wanted"**, **"Horses at the windows"** and "The Word *Progress* on my Mother's Lips doesn't ring true".

"Pockets Full of Bread" was staged at the Space Theatre in Tempe, Arizona, the National Theatre Lucian Blaga in Cluj, and the International Theatre Festival in Sibiu, Romania.

ILEANA ALEXANDRA ORLICH is Professor of English and Comparative Literature, Director of Romanian Studies, and Head of German, Romanian and Slavic Faculty in the School of International Letters and Cultures at Arizona State University. She is also a well known speaker on cultural, political and gender relations, nationalism and ethnic conflict, and theatre and politics at international conferences and symposia in China, South Korea, the Czech Republic, Hungary, Canada, Italy, France, Spain, Turkey, the UK and Romania.

In 2006 she received a National Endowment for the Arts Fellowship for Literary Translation. She was a Fulbright Professor in Romania (2006-7) and a Fulbright Senior Specialist grantee in 2011. In recent years she has been the recipient of grant awards from Romania's Cultural Institute, Romania's Writers' Union, and various organizations from the UK and the European Union. In 2005 she was awarded Romania's highest cultural recognition, Meritul Cultural al Romaniei, and, since 2010, she serves as Honorary Consul General of Romania in Arizona.

Her scholarly books include *Silent Bodies: (Re)Discovering the Women of Romanian Short Fiction* (New York: Columbia Press, 2002); *Articulating Gender, Narrating the Nation: Allegorical Femininity in Romanian Fiction* (New York: Columbia Press, 2005); *Myth and Modernity in the Twentieth-Century Romanian Novel* (New York: Columbia Press, 2009); and *Avantgardism, Politics, and the Limits of Interpretation: Reading Gellu Naum's Zenobia* (Bucuresti: Paideia Press, 2010).

Her scholarly articles have appeared in numerous international journals and edited volumes, and she is a well-known translator of Romanian and English literature. She also wrote stage adaptations in English and French of the Romanian avant-garde and contemporary theatre for performances in Romania, France and the United States and is a frequent theatre critic and commentator for Romanian literary journals.